lonely planet

Pocket
BEIJING

TOP SIGHTS • LOCAL LIFE • MADE EASY

D1053765

David Eimer

In This Book

QuickStart Guide

Your keys to understanding the city – we help you decide what to do and how to do it

Need to Know
Tips for a smooth trip

Neighbourhoods
What's where

Explore Beijing

The best things to see and do, neighbourhood by neighbourhood

Top Sights
Make the most of your visit

Local Life
The insider's city

The Best of Beijing

The city's highlights in handy lists to help you plan

Best Walks
See the city on foot

Beijing's Best...
The best experiences

Survival Guide

Tips and tricks for a seamless, hassle-free city experience

Getting Around
Travel like a local

Essential Information
Including where to stay

Our selection of the city's best places to eat, drink and experience:

- ◉ **Sights**
- ✖ **Eating**
- ⊖ **Drinking**
- ✪ **Entertainment**
- 🔒 **Shopping**

These symbols give you the vital information for each listing:

☎ Telephone Numbers	👪 Family-Friendly
⊙ Opening Hours	🐾 Pet-Friendly
🅿 Parking	🚌 Bus
🚭 Nonsmoking	⛴ Ferry
@ Internet Access	Ⓜ Metro
📶 Wi-Fi Access	Ⓢ Subway
🥗 Vegetarian Selection	🚋 Tram
📖 English-Languag Menu	🚆 Train

Find each listing quickly on maps for each neighbourhood:

Bianyifang

7 ✖ Map p52, C2

Less touristy than the o
options in the area, Bian
heritage that dates back
he Qing emperor Xia
here are roasted in
a closed oven,
n one where t
宜坊烤鸭店; and the meat
ai Dajie 崇文门外
World Shopping
期三层: roast duck

Lonely Planet's Beijing

Lonely Planet Pocket Guides are designed to get you straight to the heart of the city.

Inside you'll find all the must-see sights, plus tips to make your visit to each one really memorable. We've split the city into easy-to-navigate neighbourhoods and provided clear maps so you'll find your way around with ease. Our expert authors have searched out the best of the city: walks, food, nightlife and shopping, to name a few. Because you want to explore, our 'Local Life' pages will take you to some of the most exciting areas to experience the real Beijing.

And of course you'll find all the practical tips you need for a smooth trip: itineraries for short visits, how to get around, and how much to tip the guy who serves you a drink at the end of a long day's exploration.

It's your guarantee of a really great experience.

Our Promise

You can trust our travel infor-mation because Lonely Planet authors visit the places we write about, each and every edition. We never accept freebies for positive coverage, so you can rely on us to tell it like it is.

QuickStart Guide 7

Explore Beijing 21

Worth a Trip:

TAO IMAGES LIMITED/GETTY IMAGES ©

QuickStart Guide

Welcome to Beijing

Capital of the country everyone is talking about, Beijing seethes with a unique, fizzing energy that's utterly infectious. The city is an extraordinary clash of the distant past and supercharged present, where imperial palaces and sublime temples co-exist with stunning new architecture and avant-garde art. Beijing is also a food and shopping heaven. Whatever your tastes, there's something here for you.

National Centre for the Performing Arts (NCPA; p65), designed by architect Paul Andreu
TAO IMAGES LIMITED/GETTY IMAGES ©

Beijing
Top Sights

The Forbidden City 故宫 (p24)

Walk in the footsteps of emperors at this utterly unmissable complex that contains the best-preserved collection of ancient architecture in all of China.

The Great Wall 长城 (p106)

The very symbol of China; nothing beats climbing the steep ramparts for the breathtaking, iconic view of this fortification snaking away across the hills into the far distance.

The Summer Palace 颐和园 (p96)

Do as the Chinese royals did and escape the heat at this beautiful collection of pavilions, temples and gardens. Great views over Beijing from the top of Longevity Hill.

Temple of Heaven Park 天坛公园 (p50)

The ultimate expression of Ming dynasty architecture; stunning temples and halls with enough symbolic significance to keep an amateur necromancer busy for years.

Tiananmen Square 天安门广场 (p30)

People-watch at the world's largest public square. Catch the daily flag-raising at sunrise, and then return at sunset when the vast concrete space is at its most evocative.

Hutong 胡同 (p46)

Getting lost in the *hutong*, enchanting ancient alleyways, is absolutely essential. It's by far the best way to experience the capital's street life in all its frenetic, fun and fascinating glory.

KYLIE MCLAUGHLIN/GETTY IMAGES ©

LUIS CASTANEDA INC./GETTY IMAGES ©

798 Art District 艺术新区 (p72)

China's contemporary art boom began at this one-time factory. The art on display is innovative and ingenious, and sometimes infuriating, but never boring.

Lama Temple 雍和宫 (p34)

One of the most magnificent Tibetan Buddhist monasteries outside of the Land of Snows; join monks and locals who pray daily at this one-time imperial palace.

Beihai Park 北海公园 (p58)

Beijingers flock to this former playground of the emperors to kick back. Go boating on the lake, try the group dancing, or just watch the parade of humanity go by.

Panjiayuan Antique Market 潘家园古玩市场 (p86)

The best place in Beijing for arts, crafts and antiques, this raucous weekend market will delight shopaholics and treasure-hunters alike. Just make sure to bargain hard.

Beijing Local Life

Insider tips to help you find the real city

Ticked off Beijing's top sights? Then it's time to plunge into the city proper and start seeing how the locals live. From eating to shopping, here's how to become a temporary Beijinger.

A Night Out on Ghost Street (p36)

▶ restaurants

For a close-up look at how Beijingers treat their restaurants as party venues, take a trip to buzzing Ghost St one evening. The restaurants here are always jammed with locals doing what they do best: eating, drinking and making merry in as big and noisy a group as possible.

Step Back in Time in Dashilar (p60)

▶ ancient alleyways
▶ shopping

A great area to get lost in, Dashilar and its surrounding *hutong* offer a genuine taste of old Beijing. Browse some of the most historic shops in the city and absorb the atmosphere of a traditional Beijing neighbourhood.

Sip Cocktails in Sanlitun (p74)

▶ bars
▶ nightclubs

Brush off the dust from the palaces and temples and join Beijing's beautiful people in the nightlife zone of Sanlitun, where you can drink and dance the night away in the capital's most sophisticated bars and clubs.

Shop Like a Beijinger (p88)

▶ markets
▶ shops

Nothing gets the locals' blood flowing more than haggling over an accessory, ornament or latest must-have item of clothing. Shopping is an art form in Beijing, and the markets and shops of South Chaoyang are the places to practise it.

Ghost Street (p36)

Alleyway, Dashilar (p60)

Other great places to experience the city like a local:

Drum & Bell Tower Square (p40)

Nanluogu Xiang (p42)

Houhai (p64)

Maliandao Tea Market (p69)

Shopping Mall Restaurants (p79)

Karaoke (p80)

Ritan Park (p91)

High Life (p93)

Ethnic eats in Weigongcun (p105)

Wudaokou (p102)

Beijing
Day Planner

Day One

Only one day in Beijing? Then fight that jetlag and be out of bed in time to catch the flag-raising ceremony at **Tiananmen Square** (p30), the symbolic heart of the Chinese universe. Wander just south of the square for a breakfast snack from a street vendor, before being first in line when the astonishing **Forbidden City** (p24) opens at 8.30am. Spend the morning checking out the palace, and try to take in some of its less-visited exhibitions of imperial treasures.

After a lunch of delicious dumplings at **Duyichu** (p55), dive into the historic shopping and *hutong* neighbourhood of **Dashilar** (p60). From there, it's a short hop by subway or taxi to the **Temple of Heaven Park** (p50). Marvel at the peerless temples, the ultimate in Ming dynasty architecture, and take a breather in the shade of the ancient cypress trees that line the park.

It's time for Peking duck! Head to **Beijing Dadong Roast Duck Restaurant** (p42) for a superb introduction to the capital's most famous dish. Round the evening off with a cocktail at **Apothecary** (p79) or **Migas** (p79) in Sanlitun, Beijing's nightlife hub.

Day Two

Two days in Beijing means a trip to the **Great Wall** (p106), China's most iconic monument. It's not visible from space, despite claims to the contrary, but travel two hours or less from Beijing and you'll be standing right on it. If you're pushed for time, then head to the **Badaling** section, which can be done in a half-day. But if your schedule allows for it, try **Simatai**, which offers steep climbs and dizzying descents.

Follow a late lunch at **Najia Xiaoguan** (p91), where the recipes come straight out of the old imperial cookbook, with an afternoon of shopping in **South Chaoyang** (p88), where you can haggle to your heart's content at the likes of the **Silk Market** (p88).

After such an energetic day, sit back and let someone else do the work by catching one of Beijing's spectacular acrobatics shows at the **Chaoyang Theatre** (p81) or the less-touristy **Tianqiao Acrobatics Theatre** (p67). Then head for a well-deserved dinner at **Lost Heaven** (p55), which serves up fine folk cuisine from China's southwest in the elegant surroundings of the former Legation Quarter.

Short on time?
We've arranged Beijing's must-sees into these day-by-day itineraries to make sure you see the very best of the city in the time you have available.

Day Three

☀ If your third day in town falls on a Saturday or Sunday, head to the **Panjiayuan Antique Market** (p86) at dawn to try to outwit the antique dealers. Otherwise, hop the subway to the **Summer Palace** (p96) and spend the morning roaming its delightful gardens, temples and pavilions.

☀ Stop off for lunch in the happening student district of **Wudaokou** (p102), before travelling on to the **798 Art District** (p72). Browse the galleries, taking a break in one of the many cafes in the area, and discover for yourself what the Chinese contemporary art boom is all about.

☽ You could catch an early-evening Peking opera show at the **Huguang Guild Hall** (p68), the most atmospheric venue in town to see Beijing's local art form. Alternatively, spoil yourself with a soothing massage at the **Dragonfly Therapeutic Retreat** (p42). Afterwards, join the crowds of happy diners at one of the many hotpot restaurants on **Ghost St** (p36).

Day Four

☀ Time for some temple-hopping. Start at the **Lama Temple** (p34), a grandiose former imperial palace and Beijing's most popular Buddhist place of worship. Nearby, the serene **Confucius Temple** (p40) offers a tranquil escape from Beijing's frenetic streets.

☀ Lunch at the **Vineyard Café** (p43), a favourite with Western expats, or, for a more esoteric experience, try the **Baihe Vegetarian Restaurant** (p43), where the dishes are works of art masquerading as meat and seafood. Afterwards, meander through the *hutong* surrounding the **Drum & Bell Towers** (p40), before making your way to nearby **Beihai Park** (p58), where Beijingers come to play.

☽ You haven't come close to exhausting Beijing's after-dark options. Start the night at either **Dali Courtyard** (p42) or **Source** (p43), which both serve up fine food in the romantic setting of restored courtyard houses. Then grab a cocktail at **Mao Mao Chong** (p44) before hitting the bars in the humming *hutong* of **Nanluogu Xiang** (p42). Alternatively, check out local bands at **Yugong Yishan** (p44).

Need to Know

For more information, see Survival Guide (p135)

Currency
Renminbi (Yuan: ¥)

Language
Mandarin

Visas
All visitors to China, except for citizens of Brunei, Japan and Singapore, need a visa to enter. Standard 30-day single-entry tourist visas readily available from Chinese embassies and consulates worldwide.

Money
Most ATMs accept foreign ATM cards and credit cards. Changing foreign currency is straightforward. Credit cards are not widely accepted, except at high-end hotels, restaurants and shops.

Mobile Phones
Most foreign phones will work (check they're unlocked for roaming before you go). Local SIM cards are cheap and easy to buy.

Time
China (GMT/UTC plus eight hours)

Plugs & Adaptors
Plugs either have two or three pins (see p139); electrical current is 220V/50Hz. Adaptors can be bought at the airport.

Tipping
Tipping is not standard. High-end restaurants will add a service charge, but tips are not expected by wait staff or taxi drivers.

 Before You Go

Your Daily Budget

Under ¥300
▶ Dorm bed ¥50–70
▶ Eat street food and in local restaurants
▶ Travel by bike or public transport
▶ Visit the free sights

Midrange ¥300–600
▶ Standard double room ¥250–350
▶ Eat in a mix of restaurants, drink in bars
▶ Travel by taxi
▶ See all the sights

Top end over ¥600
▶ Room in a courtyard hotel ¥700–1000
▶ Dine in the best Chinese and international restaurants, drink in cocktail bars
▶ Tickets for shows

Useful Websites

Lonely Planet (www.lonelyplanet.com /china/beijing) Destination information, hotel booking and travel tips.

The Beijinger (www.thebeijinger.com) Entertainment listings.

Wild Wall (www.wildwall.com) All about the Great Wall.

ChinaSmack (www.chinasmack.com) Find out what China's netizens are talking about.

Advance Planning

Three months Research Beijing, book flights and get your visa.

One month Reserve your hotel.

② Arriving in Beijing

Most travellers arrive at Beijing's Capital International Airport (www.en.bcia.com .cn), which is connected to the city's subway system via the Airport Express train. International arrivals by train are at either the main Beijing Train Station or Beijing West Train Station.

✈ From Beijing Capital International Airport

Destination	Best Transport
South Chaoyang & the CBD	Airport Shuttle Bus Line 1
Dongcheng North	Airport Express
Beihai Park & Xicheng	Airport Express, then subway
North Chaoyang	Airport Express, then subway
Dongcheng South	Airport Express, then subway

At the Airport

Beijing Capital International Airport
International flights arrive at terminals 2 and 3. There are ATMs in both terminals, as well as moneychangers and information desks with English-speaking staff. You can also buy local SIM cards, pick up a temporary drivers license (at terminal 3) and hire a car. The Airport Express and Airport Shuttle buses leave from both terminals. Queues for taxis can be long, especially at terminal 3, but do not be tempted to take an illegal taxi.

③ Getting Around

Beijing is a vast, sprawling city and an increasingly traffic-clogged one. The ever-expanding subway system, though, will take you to almost everywhere you need to go. It's efficient, safe, very cheap and much quicker than sitting in a taxi most of the time. Another alternative is to do as the locals do and get on your bike.

Ⓢ Subway

Beijing's subway system gets bigger every year and is by far the best way to get around the capital. Tickets cost ¥2 for a single journey and trains run from 6am to 11pm.

⊙⊙ Cycling

Beijing is as flat as a mah jong table, which makes cycling easy. Bikes can be hired at numerous places around town and are especially good for exploring the *hutong*, where traffic is far more manageable than on the main roads.

🚗 Taxi

Taxis are plentiful in Beijing and almost all taxi drivers are honest and will use their meters. Very few, though, can speak any English and journeys can be slow because of heavy traffic. Taxi flagfall is ¥10.

🚌 Bus

Beijing's buses are numerous, go everywhere and are dirt cheap: ¥1 for a ticket. But they are always packed, move slowly and can be a challenge for non-Mandarin speakers.

Summer Palace

The Summer Palace & Haidian (p94)

Glorious gardens and parks are just a hop away from the hip student hang-out of Wudaokou.

👁 Top Sights
Summer Palace

Beihai Park & Xicheng (p56)

The parks at the heart of this historic district are some of Beijing's favourite playgrounds.

👁 Top Sights
Beihai Park

Temple of Heaven Park & Dongcheng South (p48)

Some of the finest Peking duck restaurants in the city, excellent shopping and one stunning temple.

👁 Top Sights
Temple of Heaven Park

Worth a Trip

👁 Top Sights
The Great Wall

Beijing Neighbourhoods

The Forbidden City & Dongcheng North (p22)
Imperial palaces, parks, hutong, hip bars and restaurants; this neighbourhood has it all.

◉ Top Sights
Forbidden City
Tiananmen Square
Lama Temple

North Chaoyang (p70)
Avant-garde art at the buzzing 798 Art District and cool cocktail bars in Sanlitun.

◉ Top Sights
798 Art District

South Chaoyang (p84)
Home to Beijing's best markets, as well as cutting-edge architecture.

◉ Top Sights
Panjiayuan Antique Market

798 Art District

Lama Temple

Beihai Park

Forbidden City

Tiananmen Square

Temple of Heaven Park

Panjiayuan Antique Market

Explore
Beijing

Sanlitun Village (p83)
LUIS CASTANEDA INC/GETTY IMAGES ©

Explore

The Forbidden City & Dongcheng North

With blockbuster sights such as the Forbidden City and Tiananmen Square, ancient temples, thriving *hutong,* hip bars and fabulous restaurants, Dongcheng North (东城北) is the most historic, exciting and varied neighbourhood in Beijing. You could spend all your time in the city here and still want more, so get going and dive into the district. We guarantee you won't be disappointed.

The Sights in a Day

 Catch the flag-raising ceremony at sunrise in **Tiananmen Square** (p30). Then join the locals who file reverently past Mao Zedong's mummified remains in the **Chairman Mao Memorial Hall** (p31), before being first in line when the **Forbidden City** (p24) opens. Spend the rest of the morning exploring this extraordinary complex, before exiting via the north gate and climbing the hill in **Jingshan Park** (p41) for superb views over the complex.

 After a late lunch of dumplings at **Zuo Lin You She** (p43), hop on the subway to the **Drum and Bell Towers** (p40). From there, wander east through the surrounding *hutong* (narrow alleyways) towards the **Lama Temple** (p34). Catch your breath at the peaceful **Confucius Temple** (p40).

 Tired? We hope not, as this neighbourhood jumps comes nightfall. Perhaps start the evening with Peking duck at **Beijing Dadong Roast Duck Restaurant** (p42). Alternatively, experience the delights of a traditional courtyard restaurant such as **Dali Courtyard** (p42). Afterwards, there are bars aplenty along the happening *hutong* of **Nanluogu Xiang** (p42), or live music at **Yugong Yishan** (p44).

For a night out on Ghost St, see p36.

 Top Sights

Local Life

Best of Beijing

Getting There

S Subway Line 1 to Tiananmen West or East for the Forbidden City and Tiananmen Square. Lines 2 & 5 stop at Yonghegong Lama Temple. Line 8 has a station at Shichahai for the Drum and Bell Towers.

🚍 Bus Bus 5 runs from the Drum Tower past Forbidden City to Tiananmen Square.

Top Sights
Forbidden City

Home to 24 emperors and the heart of China for 500 years, the astonishing Forbidden City (故宫; known to the locals as *Gu Gong*) is an absolute must-see for any visitor to Beijing. So-called because an unauthorised visit would result in instant death, it's both the largest palace complex in the world and the best-preserved collection of ancient architecture in China. There are 800 buildings, with 9000 rooms, as well as courtyards, pavilions and gardens, so expect to spend some time here.

👁 Map p38, A5

📞 8500 7114

www.dpm.org.cn

admission ¥60, Clock Exhibition Hall & Treasure Gallery ¥10 each

🕗 8.30am-3.30pm

Ⓢ Tiananmen East or Tiananmen West

Don't Miss

Gate of Supreme Harmony 太和门
Your first stunning sight once inside the complex is the magnificent **Gate of Supreme Harmony**, which stands guard over a huge courtyard which could hold 100,000 people. The never-ending restoration work on the palace is a huge task; note how some of the crumbling courtyard stones are stuffed with dry weeds.

Hall of Supreme Harmony 太和殿
The most important and largest structure in the Forbidden City, the **Hall of Supreme Harmony** is the first of the **Three Great Halls** (三大殿) that make up the heart of the Forbidden City. Inside is the richly decorated **Dragon Throne** from which the emperor would preside on ceremonial occasions.

Hall of Middle Harmony 中和殿
The smaller **Hall of Middle Harmony** was used as the emperor's transit lounge. Here he would make last-minute preparations, rehearse speeches and receive close ministers. On display here are two Qing dynasty sedan chairs, the emperor's mode of transport around the Forbidden City. The last Qing emperor, Puyi, used a bicycle to get around.

Hall of Preserving Harmony 保和殿
Used for banquets and later for imperial examinations, this hall has no support pillars. To its rear is a 250-tonne marble imperial carriageway carved with dragons and clouds, which was transported into Beijing on an ice path. The outer housing surrounding the Three Great Halls stored gold, silver, silks, carpets and other treasures.

☑ Top Tips

▶ Don't confuse the Gate of Heavenly Peace (p31) with the entrance to the Forbidden City. Walk on and you'll find the ticket offices.

▶ Pushy guides will approach you by the ticket office. The audio guide, which comes in 30 languages, is cheaper (¥40) and more useful.

▶ Costly rickshaw and taxi touts wait outside the north gate. Walk on a few hundred metres and catch a normal taxi.

✗ Take a Break

There are restaurants inside the complex. A better option are the delicious dumplings at **Hangzhou Xiaochi** (杭州小吃; 76 Beichang Jie; 北长街76号; dishes ¥5-10; ⊙5am-8pm; Ⓢ Tiananmen West), just west of the palace, or the American-style comfort food at **Grandma's Kitchen** (祖母的厨房; 47-2 Nanchizi Dajie; 南池子大街47-2号; dishes from ¥50; ⊙10am-10pm; Ⓢ Tiananmen East), southeast of the palace.

Clock Exhibition Hall 钟表馆

The **Clock Exhibition Hall** (admission ¥10; ⏱8.30am-4pm May-Sep, to 3.30pm Oct-Apr) is one of the highlights of the Forbidden City. The exhibition contains an astonishing array of exquisite and elaborate timepieces, mostly gifts to the Qing emperors from overseas. Time your arrival for 11am or 2pm to see the clock performance in which choice timepieces strike the hour.

Complete Palace of Peace & Longevity 宁寿全宫

A mini Forbidden City, this palace was built in the northeastern corner of the complex, mimicking the structure of the great halls of the central axis. During the Ming dynasty, this was where the Empress Dowager and the imperial concubines lived. Now it houses a number of fine exhibitions, known collectively as the **Treasure Gallery** (entrance ¥10).

Imperial Garden 御花园

At the northern end of the Forbidden City is this classical Chinese garden with 7000 sq metres of lovely landscaping, including rockeries, walkways, pavilions and ancient, carbuncular and deformed cypresses. Note the pair of **bronze elephants** whose front knees bend in an anatomically impossible fashion, signifying the power of the emperor; even elephants kowtow before him!

Understand

Concubines & Eunuchs

If ceremonial and administrative duties occupied most of the emperor's working hours, it was the pursuit of pleasure that took up his time come nightfall. According to an ancient Chinese belief, frequent sex with young girls could sustain one's youth, so the emperors sought to prolong their lives with as much frolicking with the imperial concubines as possible.

The names of the concubines were kept on jade tablets near the emperor's chambers, making it easy for the emperor to choose his companion for the night. Stripped naked (and therefore weapon-free), the lucky lady was gift-wrapped in a yellow cloth before being piggybacked over to the royal boudoir by a eunuch.

As for the palace eunuchs, the royal chop was administered using a swift knife and a special chair with a hole in the seat. Around half died after the operation. Mutilation was considered grounds for exclusion from the next life, so many eunuchs carried their former appendages around in pouches, believing that at the time of death the spirits might think them whole.

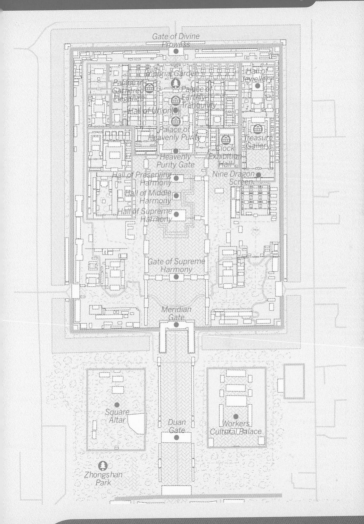

Gate of Divine Prowess

Imperial Garden

Hall of Jewellery

Palace of Gathered Elegance

Palace of Earthly Tranquility

Hall of Union

Palace of Heavenly Purity

Treasure Gallery

Heavenly Purity Gate

Clock Exhibition Hall

Hall of Preserving Harmony

Nine Dragon Screen

Hall of Middle Harmony

Hall of Supreme Harmony

Gate of Supreme Harmony

Meridian Gate

Square Altar

Duan Gate

Workers Cultural Palace

Zhongshan Park

Palace of Heavenly Purity 乾清宫

Less grand than the Three Great Halls, the buildings immediately behind them were more important in terms of the exercise of real power; a reflection of how in China power lies at the back door, or gate. Thus, the **Palace of Heavenly Purity** was a residence of Ming and early Qing emperors, and later an audience hall for receiving foreign envoys and high officials.

Hall of Union 交泰殿

Immediately behind the Palace of Heavenly Purity, the **Hall of Union** contains a clepsydra – a water clock made in 1745 with five bronze vessels and a calibrated scale. There's also a mechanical clock built in 1797 and a collection of imperial jade seals on display.

Palace of Earthly Tranquility 坤宁宫

As its name suggests, this hall was concerned with less high-minded pleasures. During the Ming dynasty, it was the home of the empress. Later, it acted as the site where the emperors got married and then as the imperial couple's bridal chamber. But that lasted for only two days; after that the empress moved out and the palace harem moved in.

Palace of Gathered Elegance 储秀宫

The last emperor, Puyi, lived in the buildings on the western side of the Forbidden City (as part of his efforts to bring the palace into the modern age, he installed a tennis court). The **Palace of Gathered Elegance** was where he resided as a child and now contains some interesting photos of Puyi.

Guardian Lions 石狮

Pairs of stone lions guard important buildings around the palace, with two particularly fine specimens in front of the **Gate of Supreme Harmony**. The male has a paw placed on a globe (representing the emperor's power over the world). The female has her paw on a baby lion (representing the fertility of the emperor's court).

Roof Guardians 蹲兽

On the corners of the roofs of halls, as with other buildings in the city, you'll see a procession of mythical creatures leading and protecting the imperial dragon, which lies at the tail end of the line. The more important the building, the more mythical beasts in the procession, with nine being the maximum.

Understand

The Forbidden City Through Time

On the site of a palace dating back to Kublai Khan, the Ming emperor Yongle established the basic layout of the Forbidden City between 1406 and 1420, basing it on the now-ruined Ming dynasty palace in Nanjing. Some estimates say the grandiose emperor employed a million labourers and craftspeople to build it. The palace lay at the heart of the old Imperial City and the wall enclosing it – assembled from 12 million bricks – is the last intact surviving city wall in Beijing.

The Pleasure Dome

The gargantuan complex sheltered two dynasties of emperors, the Ming and the Qing, who didn't stray from their pleasure dome unless they absolutely had to. A stultifying code of rules, protocol and superstition deepened its otherworldliness, perhaps typified by its twittering eunuchs. From here the emperors governed China, often erratically or incompetently. Given their isolation from the rest of the country, it's amazing that it wasn't until 1911 that revolution came knocking at the huge doors, bringing with it the end of imperial rule.

Post-1911

During the imperial era, fire was the biggest threat to the palace. Most of the buildings visitors see now are post-18th century: the largely wooden palace complex was a tinderbox and a few stray fireworks combined with a sudden gust of Gobi Desert wind could send flames dancing through it in moments.

In more recent times, looters and political extremists have proved equally dangerous. Both the invading Japanese and the Kuomintang, the Nationalist rivals to the Communist Party, took their pick of the palace's treasures on either side of WWII. Many of the most valuable artefacts are now on display in Taiwan, where the Nationalists fled after the communist victory in 1949.

The Cultural Revolution of the 1960s and '70s saw the palace become a target for the fanatical Red Guards. In a sign of how central the Forbidden City is to the Chinese psyche, then premier Zhou Enlai stepped in to prevent it being attacked, an indication of how the Forbidden City is still seen by many as representing the pinnacle of Chinese civilisation.

Top Sights
Tiananmen Square

The world's largest public square and now the very centre of the Chinese universe, Tiananmen Square (天安门广场; *Tiananmen Guangchang*) in its current incarnation was conceived by Mao Zedong as a monument to the omnipotence of the Communist Party. The huge expanse of concrete – all 440,000 sq metres of it – is certainly awe-inspiring, even if stringent security means it is not the most relaxing place. But there's more than enough room to shake a leg and the views can be breathtaking, especially at night when the square is illuminated.

👁 Map p38, A8

admission free

Ⓢ Tiananmen West, Tiananmen East or Qianmen

Don't Miss

Flag-raising/Lowering Ceremonies

Hugely popular with domestic tourists and an undeniably eye-catching spectacle are the daily flag-raising and lowering ceremonies. At sunrise and sunset, a crack squad of People's Liberation Army (PLA) soldiers march through the Gate of Heavenly Peace and onto the square at precisely 108 paces per minute, 75cm per pace, before raising or lowering the Chinese flag that flies over the square.

Gate of Heavenly Peace 天安门

Adorned with a huge portrait of Mao, this double-eaved **gate** (admission ¥15; bag storage ¥2-6; ⊙8.30am-4.30pm) to the north of the square gives its name, *Tiananmen,* to the square. Built in the 15th century and restored in the 17th, it's guarded by two pairs of Ming **stone lions**. You can climb the gate for excellent views of the square, and there's a good photo exhibition here, too.

National Museum of China 中国国际博物馆

After years of renovation, China's premier **museum** (admission free with passport; ⊙9am-5pm Tue-Sun) has finally reopened. Housed in an immense, Stalinist-style building on the eastern side of the square, it was still a work in progress at the time of writing, but the **Ancient China** exhibition on the basement floor is outstanding, while the **Bronze Art** and **Buddhist Sculpture** galleries are also impressive.

Chairman Mao Memorial Hall 毛主席纪念堂

One of the few freebies in Beijing is the chance to see the preserved body of the Great Helmsman, who is laid out in a crystal cabinet in this **memorial hall** (admission free with passport, bag storage ¥2-10, camera storage ¥2-5; ⊙8am-noon Tue-Sun) towards the

☑ Top Tips

▶ If you're coming to the dawn flag-raising/lowering ceremonies, get here as early as you can as it can get very crowded.

▶ Bikes are banned from the square; you'll be stopped if you try to ride across it. Stash cycles at the bike park to the west of the Gate of Heavenly Peace.

▶ Avoid Tiananmen Square on public holidays, especially National Day on the 1 October; it is packed to the gills and you won't be able to move.

✕ Take a Break

Head south of the square to the restored shopping street of Qianmen Dajie for delectable dumplings at **Duyichu** (p55). On the same street, you'll find the **Qianmen Quanjude Roast Duck Restaurant** (p54), the capital's most famous outlet for Peking duck.

south of the square. Reverent domestic tourists file past in their droves, so be respectful. Occasional maintenance means that Mao's body isn't always here. The compulsory bag check is across the street.

Front Gate 前门

The **Front Gate** (admission ¥20; 🕑9am-4pm Tue-Sun; **S** Qianmen), or *Qianmen,* at the south of the square actually consists of two gates, which once formed part of the old inner city walls. The northernmost gate is the 40m-high **Zhengyang Gate**, which can be climbed for decent views of the square and has a fascinating exhibition of historical photos. Directly south is **Zhengyang Gate Arrow Tower**, which you can't climb.

Great Hall of the People 人民大会堂

The venue of China's legislature, the National People's Congress (NPC), the **Great Hall of the People** (admission ¥30, bag deposit ¥2-5; 🕑8.30am-3pm), to the west of the square, is open to the public when the NPC isn't in session. The tour includes the 10,000-seat auditorium with the familiar red star embedded in a galaxy of ceiling lights. The ticket office is down the south side of the building.

Monument to the People's Heroes 人民英雄纪念碑

Right in the centre of the square, this monument was completed in 1958. The 37.9m-high granite obelisk bears bas-relief carvings of key patriotic and revolutionary events, as well as calligraphy from communist bigwigs Mao Zedong and Zhou Enlai. Mao's eight-character flourish proclaims 'Eternal Glory to the People's Heroes'. At night, the monument is illuminated.

Socialist Realist Architecture

Like every other newly communist country, the People's Republic of China took its early architectural cues from the old Soviet Union. Beijing abounds with structures built in what is known as the Socialist Realist style, but Tiananmen Square has some of the most prominent examples. Check out the 1959 **Great Hall of the People**; the architecture is monolithic and intimidating and a very fitting symbol of China's political inertia.

Understand
Tiananmen & Modern China
- -

It's no exaggeration to say that modern China was born in Tiananmen Square. On 4 May 1919, students from Peking University and other colleges demonstrated in the square, decrying China's weakness in the face of the old colonial powers and calling for a stronger, less corrupt government. Those protests sparked nationwide demonstrations and are credited with boosting nationalist sentiment. The protests politicised many young Chinese who would go on to take sides in the Communist versus Nationalists civil war that dragged on until the Communist victory in 1949.

1989 Pro-democracy Protests
On the 70th anniversary of the 4 May 1919 protests Tiananmen Square was once more occupied by students from Peking University and other colleges. The 1989 protests, though, did not end happily. On 4 June, the pro-democracy demonstrators who had occupied Tiananmen Square for months were driven out by the Chinese army. While most of the students escaped unhurt, many of the ordinary Beijingers who gathered a kilometre or so away from the square to hold up the army's advance were less lucky. Estimates of the numbers killed run into the hundreds.

The Heart of China
In the West, Tiananmen is associated strongly with the 1989 protests, but in China it is a different story. Although many Chinese remember or know about what happened in June 1989, for most people Tiananmen represents the supremacy of the Communist Party. That is just what Mao intended, when he ordered its expansion after he proclaimed the founding of the People's Republic of China (PRC) from atop the Gate of Heavenly Peace in October 1949.

Since then, Tiananmen has been the site of massive displays of communist might. During the Cultural Revolution of the 1960s and '70s, up to a million people would pack into the square to listen to speeches that drove them into a frenzy. And even now, it is where the Communist Party puts on shows of its military muscle, as it did in 2009 during the 60th anniversary of the founding of the PRC.

Top Sights
Lama Temple

Beijing's foremost Buddhist shrine, the ornately decorated Lama Temple (雍和宫; *Yonghe Gong*) offers a profound and very eye-catching introduction to Tibetan Buddhism. This former imperial palace became a temple in 1744, and is now *the* popular place of worship for the locals. There are five main halls to wander through, prayer wheels to spin (propel them clockwise), multicoloured glazed tiles, magnificent Chinese lions and tantric statuettes, all adding up to a sumptuous treat of a temple.

👁 Map p38, C1

Yonghegong Dajie; 雍和宫大街

adult ¥25, audio guide ¥50

🕐 9am-4.30pm

Ⓢ Yonghegong Lama Temple

Don't Miss

Wanfu Pavilion 万福阁

The last of the five main halls holds the temple's true highlight: a stupendous 18m-tall statue of the Maitreya Buddha in his Tibetan form, reputedly sculpted from a single block of sandalwood and which is clothed in yellow satin. Each of the statue's toes is the size of a pillow! Behind the statue is the **Vault of Avalokiteshvar**, from where a blue-faced statue of Guanyin peeks out.

Side-hall Exhibitions

There's a superb collection of bronze Tibetan Buddhist statues within **Jietai Lou**, most of which date from the Qing dynasty. The exhibits range from languorous renditions of Green Tara and White Tara to exotic, tantric pieces (such as Samvara) and figurines of the fierce-looking Mahakala. Also peruse the Tibetan Buddhist ornaments within the **Banchan Lou**: there's a fantastic array of sceptres, mandalas and tantric figures.

Yongyou Hall 永佑殿

With statues of the Buddha of Longevity and the Buddha of Medicine (to the left), this hall is especially popular with worshippers. Peek into the **East Side Hall** for its esoteric gathering of cobalt-blue Buddhas and two huge dog-like creatures. Note how the tantric statues have been partially draped to disguise their couplings.

Hall of the Wheel of Law 法轮殿

The fourth hall houses a large bronze statue of a benign and smiling Tsongkhapa (1357–1419), founder of the Yellow Hat sect of Tibetan Buddhism (which the temple belongs to), robed in yellow and illuminated from a skylight above. Also within the hall is a throne that seated the Dalai Lama when he lectured here.

☑ Top Tips

▸ Guides loiter by the entrance and ticket office, but they cost more than the audio tour that's available.

▸ Get here as early as you can, and preferably on a weekday, because the temple attracts hordes of sightseers and worshippers.

▸ The surrounding streets are jammed with shops selling incense sticks and all manner of Buddhist statues and paraphernalia. This is also a good area in which to get your fortune told!

✕ Take a Break

There are many places nearby where you can grab a breather. Try the **Vineyard Café** (p43) for excellent Western food, as well as coffee and proper English tea. Also within walking distance is the **Baihe Vegetarian Restaurant** (p43), one of the finest veggie eateries in Beijing.

Local Life
A Night Out on Ghost Street 簋街

One of the most buzzing streets in all Beijing is Ghost St (*Gui Jie; Map p38, D2;* S*Dongzhimen*), a section of Dongzhimennei Dajie. Jammed with over 150 restaurants, it attracts everyone from hipsters to office workers, man-bag-toting businessmen and families, as well as the odd celebrity. It never closes, and from sundown to sunrise Ghost St is the perfect place to join the locals as they let off steam or wind down after work.

❶ What's in a Name?

You can't miss the start of Ghost St. Officially a strip of Dongzhimennei Dajie (东直门内大街), it's lined with hundreds of swaying red lanterns. The street gets its unusual moniker from the large statue of an ancient bronze food vessel that stands at the far eastern end of Dongzhimennei Dajie, the name of which is pronounced the same as the Mandarin word for a ghost.

❷ The Ghost Street Vibe

Beijingers don't stand on ceremony when it comes to their favourite pastime of eating with as noisy and loud a group of people as possible. The fun starts outside the restaurants, where boisterous crowds wait for a table, while restaurant workers line the street trying to entice passing cars to stop. Inside, the decibel level goes through the roof as people sit around circular tables devouring food and beers at a rate of knots, while the sweating staff try to keep up with the demand.

❸ Xiao Yu Shan 小渔山

Hands-down one of the busiest places on Ghost St is this giant **joint** (☎6401 9899; 195 Dongzhimennei Dajie; 东直门内大街195号; ⏱10.30am-6am; 🅿), where crowds are always waiting for the chance to crack crayfish or gobble shrimp. Apart from seafood, it's an excellent late-night/early-morning munchies option, as it does lamb skewers and other great beer snacks, too.

❹ Little Sheep 小肥羊

Ghost St is best known for hotpot, a dish that arrived in Beijing with the invading Mongol hordes in the early 13th century. You gather around a steaming pot of flavoursome broth, add the meat and veggies of your choice, with dipping sauces on the side, and away you go. **Little Sheep** (☎8400 1669; 209 Dongzhimennei Dajie; 东直门内大街209号; ⏱9am-4am; 🅿) is a great place to sample traditional hotpot; its lamb is sourced from Inner Mongolia and all the ingredients are fresh.

❺ Chongqing Kongliang Huoguo 重庆孔亮火锅

Fire fiends will want to try the Chongqing version of hotpot at this long-standing **eatery** (☎8404 4097; 218 Dongzhimennei Dajie; 东直门内大街218号; ⏱9.30am-3am; 🅿). Indelibly associated with the southwestern city it takes its name from, this version of hotpot is eaten in exactly the same way as the Mongolian one, only with far more spices. It's fantastic on a cold winter day.

❻ Hua Jia Yi Yuan 花家怡园

More upmarket than many Ghost St eateries, **Hua Jia Yi Yuan** (☎6405 1908; 235 Dongzhimennei Dajie; 东直门内大街235号; ⏱10.30am-4am; 🅿) has a lovely setting in a courtyard house with a conservatory-style roof. The huge menu runs the gamut of China's cuisines, from Cantonese to Peking duck.

Dongzhong Jie

东直门北大街 Dongzhimen Beidajie

Chaoyangmen Beidaj

500 m
0.25 miles

Dongsi Shitiao

Dongzhimen
东直门

Nanguan Park

环北路

Poly Art Museum

Dongsishitiao Lu

For reviews see

Top Sights p24
Sights p40
Eating p42
Drinking p44
Entertainment p44

Dongzhimen Beixiaojie

Dongzhimen Nanxiaojie

Dongsi Liutiao

North 2nd Ring Rd

Dongzhimennei Dajie

Lama Temple

Yonghegong
Lama Temple
雍和宫

Xilou Hutong
Beixintiao Santiao Hutong

Dongzhimennei Dajie

Zhangzizhonglu

Zhangzizhonglu
张自忠路

Yonghegong Dajie
雍和宫大街

Dongsi Beidajie

Dongsi Beidajie 东四北大

Beixinqiao
北新桥

Confucius Temple &
Imperial College

Wudaoying Hutong

Guozijian Jie

Zhangzizhong Lu

National
Art Museum
(Meishuguan)

Andingmen
安定门

North 2nd Ring Rd
二环北路

Andingmennei Dajie

Jiaodaokou Nandajie
交道口南大街

Meishuguan Houjie

Xiaojingchang
Hutong

Beiluogu Xiang

Doufuchi Hutong

Beiluogu Xiang
北锣鼓巷

Dongmianhua Hutong

Banchang Hutong

Dongmianhua Hutong

Donghuangchengen Beijie

Beiheyan Da

Mao'er Hutong

Di'anmen Dongdajie
地安门东大街

Nanluoguxiang
南锣鼓巷

Shatanbei Jie

Zhonglouwan Hutong

Baochao Hutong

Gulou Dongdajie
鼓楼东大街

Nanluogu Xiang

Shichahai

Drum
Tower

Shichahai
什刹海

Di'anmenwai
Dajie

Di'anmenwai Dajie
地安门外大街

Jingshan Hou

Huicheng River (City Moat)

Sights

Drum Tower

HISTORIC BUILDING

1   Map p38, A2

Dominating the area, the drum tower dates back to 1272 (although it has been re-built since) and provides a great view over the surrounding area. The drums were beaten here hourly in ancient times to keep the proles punctual, and there are still daily drumming performances (hourly from 9.30am to 4.45pm). The Bell Tower is just to the north. (鼓楼; Gulou Dongdajie 鼓楼东大街; admission ¥20, combined ticket with Bell Tower ¥30; ⏰entry 9am-4.40pm; Ⓢ Shichahai)

◯ Local Life

Dance in the Shadow of the Drum Tower

The small square between the Drum and Bell Towers is great for people-watching. Come nightfall, the towers are lit up beautifully and the locals from the nearby *hutong* come out to play. Especially fun is the formation dancing. It's very informal and strangers are welcomed. When you're done with twirling around, grab a drink at the **Drum and Bell** (鼓钟咖啡馆; 41 Zhonglouwan Hutong; 钟楼湾胡同41号; beers from ¥15, cocktails from ¥35; ⏰1pm-2am), which sits between the two towers and has a fine roof terrace in the summer.

Bell Tower

HISTORIC BUILDING

2 ◎ Map p38, A2

The tower was first constructed in 1272, but felled numerous times by fire; its present structure dates from 1745, although it looks noticeably more ancient that the neighbouring Drum Tower, which is just to the south. Climb up the steep steps (carefully) to gawk at the 63-tonne bell and for a sweeping panorama over the surrounding *hutong*. (钟楼; 9 Zhonglouwan Hutong 钟楼湾胡同9号; admission ¥20, combined ticket with Drum Tower ¥30; ⏰9am-4.40pm; Ⓢ Shichahai)

Confucius Temple & Imperial College

TEMPLE

3 ◎ Map p38, C1

China's second-largest Confucian temple makes for a super sanctuary from the chaos and noise of Beijing's streets. Wander through the pavilions (note the mythical dragonlike creatures on the roofs), before strolling next door to the former Imperial College, where emperors presented Confucian classics to rapt audiences of students and scholars. (孔庙与国子监; 13 Guozijian Jie 国子监13号; admission ¥30; ⏰8.30am-5.30pm; Ⓢ Yonghegong Lama Temple)

Poly Art Museum

MUSEUM

4 ◎ Map p38, E3

An arm of the government, the Poly Group set up this small but exquisite museum to house the incredible bronzes and stone Buddhist effigies (some amazingly still have their pig-

Bell Tower

ment on them) it has spent much time and money buying at international auctions, after they were pillaged during China's turbulent past. It's an amazing collection. (保利艺术博物馆; www.polymuseum.com; 9th fl, Poly Plaza, 14 Dongzhimen Nandajie 东直门南大街14号; admission ¥20; ⊙9.30am-4.30pm; Ⓢ Dongsi Shitiao)

Beijing Police Museum   MUSEUM

5 ◉ Map p38, B8

Housed in a historic colonial-era building (a former American bank), this museum offers a fascinating insight into the Beijing underworld in all its seamy, scurrilous glory: brothels, opium dens, class traitors, spies and serial killers. There are plenty of English captions, as well as uniforms, weapons (there's a mini shooting range on the 4th floor) and gruesome crime-scene photos. (北京警察博物馆; 36 Dongjiaomin Xiang 东交民巷36号; admission ¥5; ⊙9am-4pm Tue-Sun; Ⓢ Qianmen)

Jingshan Park   PARK

6 ◉ Map p38, A5

One of our favourite parks, and one of the few places in Beijing where you'll see a hill. It's man-made (built to protect the neighbouring Forbidden City from evil spirits using earth excavated during the construction of its moat), but climb it for tremendous views over the centre of the city. (景山公园; Jingshan Qianjie; admission ¥2; ⊙6am-9.30pm; Ⓢ Tiananmen West then 🚍5)

Dragonfly Therapeutic Retreat

MASSAGE

7 Map p38, B6

The two-hour Hangover Relief Massage at this soothing, upmarket spa

 Local Life

Nanluogu Xiang

Once a traditional, sleepy alley, the 800-year old *hutong* of **Nanluogu Xiang** (Map p38, B3; §Nanluoguxiang) is now one of the most happening areas in Beijing; an insatiably bubbly strip of bars, cafes, restaurants and shops that's hugely popular with young Beijingers. You could spend the day here browsing for gifts, or the night bar-hopping. Do make sure, though, to dive into the alleys that run off Nanluogu Xiang. Some are now sprouting bars and cafes too, but many *hutong*, such as historic Mao'er Hutong, remain largely residential. You won't have to walk too far before you discover courtyard houses that have been home to the same families for generations.

Other *hutong* that are well worth a wander:

▶ Guozijian Jie, near Confucius Temple (Map p38, B1)

▶ Zhonglouwan Hutong, near the Drum Tower (Map p38, A2)

▶ Jiansuo Zuoxiang, where you'll find Mao Zedong's former home (Map p38, B5)

works wonders, but for real pampering go for the Royal Delight, in which two masseurs get to work at the same time. Foot massages, facials and manicures are also available. (悠庭保健会所; 60 Donghuamen Dajie 东华门大街60号; ⏰11am-1am; §Tiananmen East)

Eating

Dali Courtyard

YUNNAN $$$

8 Map p38, B2

Idyllic on a summer evening, when you eat at tables set around the courtyard of a restored *hutong* house, this place specialises in the delicate flavours of southwest China. There's no menu. Instead, the chef decides which five or six dishes to give you, depending on what inspires him and which ingredients are fresh. Drinks are extra. (大理; ☎8404 1430; 67 Xiaojingchang Hutong, Gulou Dongdajie 鼓楼东大街小经厂胡同67号; set menus from ¥128; ⏰11am-3pm & 6-11pm; §Andingmen)

Beijing Dadong Roast Duck Restaurant

PEKING DUCK $$$

9 Map p38, E3

A long-term favourite with Beijingers; Dadong's hallmark bird is crispy, lean and delicious. With a large and bright dining area, this is perhaps the best place to try the capital's signature dish, but book ahead so as to be prepared to wait for a table. (北京大董烤鸭店; ☎5169 0328/29; 1st fl, Nanxincang International Plaza, 22 Dongsishitiao Lu 东四十条22

号南新仓国际大厦1层; roast duck ¥238;
⏱11am-10pm; Ⓢ Dongsi Shitiao; 📖)

Tan Hua Lamb BBQ
CHINESE BARBECUE $

10 Map p38, C2

On summer nights, Beijingers take to
the *hutong* to eat and drink outside.
This is one of the most popular spots,
a raucous lamb barbecue joint where
you grill your own leg of lamb on
your own personal table-top spit and
accompany the meat with a selection
of cold dishes. Order the lamb by the
jin (500g). If the weather is cold, you
can always eat inside. (碳花烤羊腿; 63
Beixintiao Santiao Hutong 北新桥三条胡
同63号; lamb per jin ¥32, side dishes ¥1-12;
⏱11am-midnight; Ⓢ Beixinqiao)

Source
SICHUAN $$$

11 Map p38, B3

A swish Sichuan restaurant, but with
the spices and chillies toned down,
Source is a great choice for a date,
thanks to its lovely courtyard house
setting and pleasant service. You
order from set menus that change
every month. (都江园; 📞6400 3736; 14
Banchang Hutong 板厂胡同14号; meals
for 2 from ¥288; ⏱11am-2pm & 5-10pm;
Ⓢ Nanluoguxiang; 📖)

Baihe Vegetarian Restaurant
CHINESE VEGETARIAN $$

12 Map p38, D2

All Beijing's vegetarian restaurants
present dishes masquerading as meat.

Here, though, the selection – lamb
kebabs and Peking duck – is more
imaginative than usual, while the
courtyard setting is delightful. Service
is courteous and the atmosphere
relaxed. (百合素食; 📞6405 2082; 23
Caoyuan Hutong, Dongzhimennei Beixiaojie 东
直门内北小街草园胡同23号; dishes from
¥25; ⏱11.30am-3pm & 5-9.30pm; Ⓢ Dongzhimen or Beixinqiao; 😊📷📖)

Zuo Lin You She
CHINESE BEIJING $

13 Map p38, B4

This locals' favourite is a neighbourhood institution and a great place
to sample real Beijing cuisine. The
golden-fried, finger-shaped dumplings
(meat and veggie options) are the
house speciality, but the pickled fish
and spicy tofu paste are also excellent.
(左邻右舍褡裢火烧; 50 Meishuguan
Houjie 美术馆后街50号; dumplings ¥4-6,
dishes ¥5-20; ⏱11am-9.30pm; Ⓢ National Art
Museum; 📖)

Vineyard Café
WESTERN $$

14 Map p38, C1

Perfect for long, lazy weekend
brunches and equally laid-back in
the evening, the Vineyard has a nice
conservatory, sofas to sink into, and
a menu strong on salads, pizzas and
Western classics such as mussels in
white wine. It's a few minutes' walk
from the Lama Temple on an increas-
ingly trendy *hutong*. (葡萄院儿; 📞6402
7961; 31 Wudaoying Hutong 五道营胡同31
号; mains from ¥45; ⏱11.30am-11pm Tue-
Sun; Ⓢ Yonghegong Lama Temple; 😊)

Donghuamen Night Market

STREET FOOD $

15 Map p38, B6

A sight in itself, this market has dozens of stallholders who try to entice you to sample such exotic snacks as grasshoppers, scorpions and snakes. If that isn't tempting, then more conventional choices such as lamb skewers and stuffed aubergines, are available, as well as noodles and savoury pancakes. (东华门夜市; Dong'anmen Dajie 东安门大街; snacks ¥5-15; ⏱5.30-10.30pm; Ⓢ Wangfujing or Dengshikou)

Drinking

Mao Mao Chong

BAR

16 Map p38, B3

Tucked down a quiet *hutong,* there's a strong choice of cocktails available here, as well as a decent selection of beers. Nonsmoking throughout the bar. The pizzas here also get rave reviews. (毛毛虫; 12 Banchang Hutong 板厂胡同12号; beers/cocktails from ¥25/40; ⏱7pm-midnight Wed-Sun; Ⓢ Nanluoguxiang; ☻)

El Nido

BAR

17 Map p38, B1

It's a pint-sized and very busy bar (outdoor seating in the summer) that has a winning combination of a huge range of foreign brews, whiskies and absinthe, as well as its own homemade vodka; try the Sichuan shot if you need to warm up. Also does decent tapas-themed bar snacks. (59号酒吧; 59 Fangjia Hutong Dongdajie 方家胡同59号; beers from ¥10; ⏱6pm-late; Ⓢ Andingmen)

12SqM

BAR

18 Map p38, A3

Formerly Beijing's smallest bar (the clue is in the name), this friendly, relaxed place has expanded but still attracts a decent mix of expats, locals and visitors. Good selection of whiskies and beers and completely nonsmoking. (12平米; cnr Nanluogu Xiang & Fuxiang Hutong; 南锣鼓巷福祥胡同1号; beers/cocktails from ¥20/35; ⏱noon-1am; Ⓢ Nanluoguxiang; ☻)

Modernista

BAR

19 Map p38, A1

Styled on a European tapas bar, this place reels in the bohemian crowd with live music (mostly jazz) and cultural events such as film screenings, dance classes and mah jong evenings. (老摩; 44 Baochao Hutong 宝钞胡同44号; beers from ¥15; ⏱4pm-2am, closed Mon; Ⓢ Shichahai)

Entertainment

Yugong Yishan

LIVE MUSIC

20 Map p38, C3

Housed in a historic building that's reputed to be one of the most haunted in Beijing, but the sound of the local and foreign bands, solo artists and DJs who take to the stage here will

Donghuamen Night Market

drown out the screams of the ghosts. It's perhaps the best place in the city to listen to live music. (愚公移山; West Courtyard former site of Duan Qirui Government, 3-2 Zhangzizhong Lu 张自忠路3-2号段祺瑞执政府旧址西院; ☉7pm-2am; Ⓢ Zhangzizhonglu)

Shopping

Grifted   SOUVENIRS

21 🔒 Map p38, B2

Slap in the middle of trendy Nanluogu Xiang (p42), Grifted has a wide selection of tongue-in-cheek gift options, most made locally. Check out the dolls of Mao, Marx and Lenin; communist icons reinvented as soft toys. T-shirts,

Mao-print cushions, quirky lanterns and umbrellas are available, too. (贵福天地; 32 Nanluogu Xiang 南锣鼓巷32号; ☉10am-10pm; Ⓢ Nanluoguxiang)

Plastered 8   T-SHIRTS

22 🔒 Map p38, A2

Purveyors of ironic, Beijing-themed T-shirts (from ¥138) which are good to give as gifts, or to keep as mementos of your trip. Directly opposite the shop is a rare Cultural Revolution–era slogan exhorting the people to put their faith in the PLA. (创可贴T-恤; 61 Nanluogu Xiang 南锣鼓巷61号; ☉10am-10pm; Ⓢ Nanluoguxiang)

Top Sights
Hutong

Getting There

S **Subway** For the Drum Tower, take Line 8 to Shichahai.

S Lines 2 or 5 for Yonghegong Lama Temple.

S Line 2 to Qianmen for *hutong* southwest of Tiananmen Sq.

The very essence of Beijing, the *hutong* (胡同) are the ancient alleyways that cut across the centre of town. Wandering them is an essential part of any visit to the capital. Not only do these enchanting passageways offer a glimpse of what old Beijing was like, but they are still home to around 20% of the residents of the inner city. Diving into them is by far the best way to experience Beijing's intensely dramatic and unrestrained street life.

Nanluogu Xiang (p42)

Don't Miss

Cycling the Hutong

While it's easy to wander the *hutong* on foot, it's even better to do it on two wheels. With far less traffic than the main roads, the *hutong* are made for biking, and you'll wheel through far more of them than you could by walking.

Courtyard Houses 四合院

Courtyard houses, or *siheyuan,* are the building blocks of the *hutong* world. Some are now museums, but many are still occupied, although most have been subdivided and now house a number of residents, rather than just one well-off family as they did in the imperial era. The most prestigious *siheyuan* have big red doors opening onto the courtyard, or a series of courtyards, and sometimes stone lions out front.

Prince Gong's Residence 恭王府

Take a trip to this beautiful **complex** (14 Liuyin Jie 柳荫街14号; adult ¥40, tours incl opera performance & tea ceremony ¥70; ⏰ 7.30am-4.30pm mid-Mar–Oct, 8am-4pm Nov–mid-Mar; Ⓢ Ping'anli) of pavilions and gardens, perhaps Beijing's most celebrated example of a courtyard house (on a very large scale!). It was reputedly the model for the house in *Dream of the Red Mansions,* one of China's best-loved novels.

Getting Lost

Most *hutong* run east–west, although some, like Nanluogu Xiang (p42), run north–south. Many have numerous twists and turns, while others are just single lanes. A few are almost impossibly narrow, yet others are more wide and tree-lined. The only way you'll discover the sheer variety of *hutong*-land is to get lost in it. Don't worry about getting back; you're never too far from a main road.

Hutong-rich neighbourhoods lie around the Drum Tower (p40), Lama Temple (p34), west of the Forbidden City (p24) and southwest of Tiananmen Square (p30).

☑ Top Tips

▶ *Hutong* dwellers are friendly folk and the doors of their houses are often open. But that doesn't mean you can just stroll in. Always ask before you peek inside.

▶ After you've explored the *hutong* around the Drum Tower or the Lama Temple, head to nearby Nanluogu Xiang (p42), an ancient alley that's now a humming bar, restaurant and shopping zone.

✕ Take a Break

Small restaurants and cafes are scattered throughout all *hutong.* Around the Lama Temple, try the friendly, Buddhist-themed **Café Confucius** (Map p38, C2; 秀冠咖啡; 25 Guozijian Jie 国子监街25号; ⏰ 8.30am-8.30pm; 🛜).

Explore

Temple of Heaven Park & Dongcheng South

Even the most jaded temple-hopper will have their faith restored by the simply stunning Temple of Heaven (天), the highlight of compact and low-key Dongcheng South (城南), which encompasses the now defunct district of Chongwen. If that's not enough, some of the capital's finest Peking duck restaurants make their home here while there's serious shopping at the famous Hongqiao Pearl Market.

The Sights in a Day

☀ Get to the **Temple of Heaven Park** (p50) nice and early to see locals starting their day by dancing and practising taichi under the ancient and gnarled cypress trees that line this park. Then you'll be in pole position to explore the Temple of Heaven complex when it opens at 8am. Make sure to test the remarkable acoustic qualities of the Echo Wall (p50) before the crowds get there.

☀ Exit the park by the east gate and walk a few hundred metres north to the **Hongqiao Pearl Market** (p55), where five floors of pearls, jewellery and jade await you. After browsing away, hop the subway for the short ride to **Ming City Wall Ruins Park** (p53) and the **Southeast Watchtower** (p53). From there, you can wander west through the surviving *hutong* of the neighbourhood towards Qianmen.

☾ Low key it may be, but this district has some of the best and most traditional Peking duck restaurants in town, such as the **Liqun Roast Duck Restaurant** (p54). Alternatively, there are fine dining options like **Lost Heaven** (p55) in the restored former Legation Quarter.

 Top Sights

Temple of Heaven Park (p50)

♥ **Best of Beijing**

Best Food
Liqun Roast Duck Restaurant (p54)

Qianmen Quanjude Roast Duck Restaurant (p54)

Bianyifang (p55)

Best Architecture
Temple of Heaven (p50)

Southeast Watchtower (p53)

Best Markets
Hongqiao Pearl Market (p55)

Best Museums & Galleries
Red Gate Gallery (p53)

Getting There

Ⓢ **Subway** Take Line 5 to Tiantandongmen for Temple of Heaven Park and Hongqiao Pearl Market. Use the same line to travel north to Chongwenmen for Ming City Wall Ruins Park and Southeast Watchtower. Line 2 also stops at Chongwenmen, as well as at Qianmen for Peking duck restaurants and the former Legation Quarter.

Top Sights
Temple of Heaven Park

This collection of halls and altars set within a delightful park (天坛公园; *Tiantan Gongyuan*) is a perfect example of Ming architectural design. Each year, the emperors – the sons of heaven – came here to seek divine clearance and good harvests and to atone for the sins of their people in an esoteric ceremony of prayers and ritual sacrifices. Everything about the complex is unique, with shape, colour and sound combining to take on symbolic significance, while the park is a true oasis from Beijing's bedlam.

⊙ Map p52

Tiantan Donglu (天坛东路)

park only/park & te ¥15/35, audio guide (with ¥100 deposit)

⊙park 6am-9pm, te 8am-5pm

S Tiantandongmen

Gateway to the Round Altar

Don't Miss

Hall of Prayer for Good Harvests 祈年殿

The crowning structure of the complex is the supreme Hall of Prayer (*Qinian Dian*), magnificently mounted on a three-tiered marble terrace and capped with a triple-eaved umbrella roof of purplish-blue tiles. Amazingly, the wooden pillars support the ceiling without nails or cement – quite an accomplishment for a building 38m high and 30m in diameter.

Echo Wall 回音壁

This 65m structure (*Huiyin Bi*) is no ordinary wall. Its unique acoustic properties mean that a whisper will travel clearly from one end to the other. In the courtyard are the **Triple-Sounds Stones**. It is said that if you clap or shout while standing on the stones, the sound is echoed once from the first stone, twice from the second stone and thrice from the third stone.

Round Altar 圜丘坛

The 5m-high Round Altar (*Yuan Qiu Tan*) is arrayed in three tiers; its geometry revolves around the imperial number nine. Odd numbers were considered heavenly, and nine is the largest single-digit odd number. Stand in the centre of the upper terrace and say something – the sound bounces off the marble balustrades, amplifying your voice.

The Park

One of the joys of a visit here is the chance to kick back in the park itself. There are around 4000 ancient, knotted cypresses (some 800 years old, their branches propped up on poles) providing much-needed shade. Typical of Chinese parks, the wild irregularity of nature is largely eliminated, and the resulting order, balance and harmony has a somewhat haunting beauty.

☑ Top Tips

▶ There's no difference in cost between the 'through ticket' (ie park and temple) and buying the park (¥15) and temple (¥20) site tickets separately; save time by buying the through ticket.

▶ You can enter the park at any of the four gates, located on each point of the compass, but if you want to recreate the route the emperors took, start at the south gate.

✗ Take a Break

A good place to rest your legs after touring the park is **Wedome** (味多美; 12 Tiyuguan Lu 体育馆路12 号; coffee from ¥25; ⊙9am-10.30pm; ⓢTiantandongmen; ☻), which is opposite the east gate and does decent coffee and cakes. Otherwise, it's a short subway or taxi ride to the delicious dumplings at **Duyichu** (p55).

A

FORMER FOREIGN LEGATION QUARTER

Dōngdān Park

Dōngjiaomin Xiang

B

Chongwenmen 崇文门

Bĕijīng Train Station 北京火车站

C

Ming City Wall Ruins Park

D

Southea Watchtow

1
5 Qianmen Dongdajie 前门东大街

Chongwenmen Xidajie

Chongwenmen Dongdajie 崇文门东大街

Beiyangshikou

2

Xidamochang Jie
3

Dongdamochang Jie

Zhuying Hutong

Donghuashi Dajie

Qianmen Dongcelu 前门东侧路

Xixinglong Jie

Dongxinglong Jie
7

Xihuashi Dajie

2

Qinian Dajie 祈年大街

Zhushikou Dongdajie

Chongwenmennwai Dajie 崇文门外大街

Guangqumennei Dajie

Xingfu Dajie

Jinyuchi Jie

Dongxiaoshi Jie

Ciqikou 磁器口

CHÓNGWÉN

Tiantan Lu 天坛路
North Gate

Fahuasi 法华寺
8

Fahuasi Jie

3
◎ **Temple of Heaven Park**

East Gate

Tiantandongmen 天坛东门

Tiantan Donglu 天坛东路

Tiyuguan Xiu

Tiyuguan Lu

West Gate

Longtan Lu 龙潭路

Longt Pa

4

Yongdingmennei Dajie

Bĕijīng Amusement Park

Tianqiao Nandajie

South Gate

Yongdingmen Dongjie 永定门东街

Hucheng River (City Moat)

Yongdingmen Dongbinhe Lu

Jingtai Lu

Zuo'anmen Xibinhe Lu

For reviews see

5

N 0   500 m
0   0.25 miles

Sights

Ming City Wall Ruins Park

CITY WALLS

1  Map p52, D1

As late as the early 1950s, Beijing was still a walled city. Now, all that remains of the once mighty walls is this slender, restored strip within a small park. Follow the footpath that runs alongside the wall and check out the bullet holes in some of the bricks, a legacy of the 1900 Boxer Rebellion. (明城墙遗址公园; Chongwenmen Dongda-jie 崇文门东大街; admission free; ⓧ24hr; ⑤Chongwenmen)

Southeast Watchtower

HISTORIC BUILDING

2  Map p52, D1

This Ming-era watchtower has 144 archer windows but is also notable for the 'I was here' graffiti left by international troops during the 1900 Boxer Rebellion. Say you're visiting the Red Gate Gallery and you'll get into the tower for free. (东南角楼; Dongbianmen 东便门; admission ¥10; ⓧ8am-5.30pm; ⑤Jianguomen, Chongwenmen)

Red Gate Gallery

ART GALLERY

On the watchtower's first floor is the Red Gate Gallery (see 2  Map p52, D1), one of the city's most influential

© WILLAM PERRY/ALAMY ©

Southeast Watchtower

contemporary art spaces. (☎6525 1005; www.redgategallery.com; ⏱9am-5pm; ⓢJianguomen, Chongwenmen)

Eating

Liqun Roast Duck Restaurant
PEKING DUCK $$$

3 ⊗ Map p52, A1

The duck here is so prized that you have to call a day ahead to reserve both a bird and a table (otherwise, turn up at off-peak times and be prepared to wait an hour). Buried down a crumbling *hutong,* the restaurant itself has seen better days, but the duck is delicious and comes with all the trimmings. (利群烤鸭店; ☎6702 5681, 6705 5578; 11 Beixiangfeng Hutong; 前门东大街正义路南口北翔凤胡同11号; roast duck ¥220; ⏱10am-10pm; ⓢQianmen; ⏱ 📵)

Qianmen Quanjude Roast Duck Restaurant
PEKING DUCK $$$

4 ⊗ Map p52, A2

The most popular branch of Beijing's most famous destination for duck (check out the photos of everyone from Fidel Castro to Zhang Yimou), this place is geared to the tourist hordes (both domestic and foreign). But if the service is peremptory, then the duck, which is roasted in ovens fired by fruit-tree wood, is very tasty

IMAGINECHINA/CORBIS ©

Qianmen Quanjude Roast Duck Restaurant

and juicy. (前门全聚德烤鸭店; ☑6701 1379, 6511 2418; 30 Qianmen Dajie 前门大街30号; roast duck ¥228; ⏰lunch & dinner; Ⓢ Qianmen; 🅿)

Lost Heaven
CHINESE YUNNAN **$$$**

 5 Map p52, A1

With a lovely setting within the restored former legation quarter, Lost Heaven specialises in the folk cuisine of Yunnan Province in China's south-west. Try the Dai-style roast pork in banana leaf (¥68), or one of the many splendid salads. But all the dishes on the extensive menu are enticing, while there's an elegant outside area and attentive service. Book ahead. (花马天堂; ☑8516 2698; 23 Qianmen Dongdajie 前门东大街23号; dishes from ¥40; ⏰ lunch & dinner; Ⓢ Qianmen; 😊🅿)

Duyichu
CHINESE DUMPLINGS **$**

 6 Map p52, A2

A hangover from the Qing dynasty, the house speciality here are *shaomai,* the delicate dumplings that originated in eastern China. They're delightful little bundles of meat, fish or vegetables, so be prepared to queue for a table at weekends. (都一处; ☑6702 1555; 38 Qianmen Dongdajie 前门大街38号; dumplings from ¥36; ⏰9am-9pm; Ⓢ Qianmen)

Bianyifang
PEKING DUCK **$$$**

 7 Map p52, C2

Less touristy than the other duck options in the area, Bianyifang cites a heritage that dates back to the reign of the Qing emperor Xianfeng. The birds here are roasted in the *menlu* style – in a closed oven, as opposed to a half-open one where the duck hangs to cook – and the meat is nice and tender. (便宜坊烤鸭店; ☑6711 2244; 3rd fl, China New World Shopping Mall, 5 Chongwenmenwai Dajie 崇文门外大街5号新世界商场二期三层; roast duck ¥198; ⏰ lunch & dinner; Ⓢ Chongwenmen; 😊🅿)

Shopping

Hongqiao Pearl Market
MARKET

8 Map p52, C3

Home to more pearls than the South Seas, this ever-popular emporium houses its cheaper specimens on the 3rd floor. Better-quality, and more pricey, pearls can be found on the 4th and 5th floors. There's jade, jewellery, clothes and electronics too, and the roof garden offers a splendid view over the Temple of Heaven. (红桥市场; 36 Hongqiao Lu 红桥路36号; ⏰9am-7pm; Ⓢ Tiantandongmen)

Explore

Beihai Park & Xicheng

The three lakes that dominate the district of Xicheng (西城) make up one of Beijing's great playgrounds. With Beihai Park (北海公园) at the centre, they offer hours of open-air fun, from ice-skating to boating. This area, which includes the former neighbourhood of Xuanwu, is one of striking contrasts, rich with temples and *hutong*, as well as being home to the capital's oldest shops. It's impossible to be bored here.

The Sights in a Day

☀ Start the day at the **Capital Museum** (p64), Beijing's finest and *the* place to get the lowdown on local folklore. Then strike east by metro to **Liulichang**, Beijing's premier street for antiques and calligraphy. From there, it's a short stroll through the *hutong* to some of the oldest shops in Beijing.

☀ Try the famed steamed dumplings on offer at **Goubuli** (p66), before jumping back on the subway to spend the afternoon at **Beihai Park** (p58) and neighbouring **Houhai** (p64). There are temples to explore within the park, and boats to laze around on, or if it's winter hire a pair of ice skates.

☾ Cool restaurants, such as **4Corners** (p65), abound around Houhai. The south of this neighbourhood is renowned for its Peking opera and acrobatics shows, and you can't leave town without seeing one of those. The **Huguang Guild Hall** (p68) is a hugely atmospheric Peking opera venue, while the high-wire display at the **Tianqiao Acrobatics Theatre** (p67) is awesome. If you want a more relaxed evening, then join the local jazz fans at the very mellow **East Shore Jazz Café** (p68).

For a local's day in Dashilar, see p60

◉ Top Sights

Beihai Park (p58)

◯ Local Life

Step Back in Time in Dashilar (p60)

💜 Best of Beijing

Best Food
4Corners (p65)

Yuelu Shanwu (p65)

Hutong Pizza (p66)

Best Drinking & Nightlife
Bed Bar (p67)

Best Architecture
Huguang Guild Hall (p68)

Best Markets
Maliandao Tea Market (p69)

Getting There

S Subway Four subway lines cut across the neighbourhood. For Beihai Park, take Line 4 to Xisi or Line 8 to Nanluoguxiang. For Houhai, take Line 8 to Shichahai or Nanluoguxiang. Use the Muxidi stop on Line 1 for the Capital Museum and White Cloud Temple. To get to Lilulichang and Dashilar, take Line 2 to Hepingmen and Qianmen, respectively.

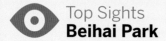

Top Sights
Beihai Park

With an extraordinary history as the former palace of the great Mongol emperor Kublai Khan, and back garden for the subsequent Yuan dynasty emperors, Beihai Park (北海公园) is an oasis for Beijingers. With the tranquil lake of Beihai at its centre and with temples, pavilions and spirit walls scattered through it, the park offers visitors a chance to combine sightseeing with fun, whether it's mucking around in a boat, having a picnic or just watching the parade of humanity that passes through.

◉ Map p62, E3

park/park & sights Apr-Oct ¥10/20, Nov-Mar ¥5/15

Pedalo hire per hour ¥80 (¥200 deposit)

⊙ 9am-9pm, sights 9am-5pm

🆂 Xisi or Nanluoguxiang

The White Dagoba on Jade Islet

Don't Miss

Jade Islet 琼华岛

Made out of the heaped earth scooped out to create Beihai Lake itself and dominated by the 36m-high **White Dagoba**, Jade Islet sits in the southeastern corner of the lake. You can reach it by a land bridge close to the southern entrance, or catch a boat (¥10) from the northwestern shore.

Yongan Temple 永安寺

The principal site on the Jade Islet is this impressive temple. The stand-out hall is the Hall of the Wheel of the Law (Falun Dian), with its central effigy of Sakyamuni. At the rear of the temple you will find a bamboo grove and a steep flight of steps leading onto more halls, before the final flight of steps brings you to the **White Dagoba** itself.

Xitian Fanjing 西天梵境

This is one of the most interesting temples in all Beijing. The **Dacizhenru Hall** (Dacizhenru Dian) dates back to the Ming dynasty and is supported by huge wooden pillars. It contains three huge statues of Sakyamuni, the Amithaba Buddha and Yaoshi Fo (Medicine Buddha). Make sure to see the nearby **Nine Dragon Screen** (Jiulong Bi), a glimmering 5m-high and 27m-long stretch of coloured glazed tiles. Xitian Fanjing is to the west of the north entrance to the park.

☑ Top Tips

▶ You can enter the park by its southern gate on Wenjin Jie, or the northern gate on Di'anmen Xidajie. But if you're planning to move onto the Houhai lakes later, it makes sense to enter from the south and exit by the north gate.

▶ This is one of the best spots in the city to see the locals practising taichi; they gather on the northern shore outside the Xitian Fanjing temple (p59).

▶ Make sure to buy the 'through ticket' (park and sights) to get you into all the park sights.

✕ Take a Break

Beihai Park is a great spot for a picnic, while neighbouring Houhai Lake is surrounded by cafes and restaurants. Try **4Corners** (p65) for meals and/or coffee breaks, or **Yuelu Shanwu** (p65) for spicy Hunan cuisine with a view over the lake.

Local Life
Step Back in Time in Dashilar

A warren of historic *hutong* southwest of Tiananmen Square (p30), centred on the ancient shopping street of Dashilar (大栅栏), this area is a fascinating throwback to old Beijing. Despite some desultory redevelopment, Dashilar retains a medieval feel. Its cramped, chaotic lanes are a mix of homes and shops, and wandering around them is a great way to experience the buzz of a traditional *hutong* neighbourhood.

1 **Qing Dynasty Shopping Mall**
The entrance to Dashilar, officially known as Dazhalan Jie (大栅栏街), is via a tiny alley off the restored Qianmen Dajie. The frenzied atmosphere of commerce is just the same as it was during the Qing dynasty, when this was Beijing's premier shopping area and each of the lanes off Dashilar was known for selling a specific product.

② **Pills & Potions**

Make sure to stop in at **Tongrentang** (同仁堂; 24 Dazhalan Jie 大栅栏街24号; ⏰8am-7.30pm; Ⓢ Qianmen), which has been peddling pills and potions since 1669. It was a royal dispensary in the Qing dynasty and its herbal medicines are based on secret remedies. If you're feeling rough, there are doctors on site for consultations. They'll cure you of anything from fright to encephalitis, or so the shop claims.

③ **Daguanlou Cinema** 大观楼影城

Dashilar evolved as a commercial area because shops were banned from the imperial city itself, along with theatres and brothels. That's why Dashilar was also the site of the first cinema in Beijing. Opened in 1903 and still showing films daily, **Daguanlou Cinema** (36 Dazhalan Jie 大栅栏街36号) is now the longest-running movie house in the world.

④ **Stinky Tofu**

Cross Meishi Jie and enter the western side of Dazhalan Jie (大栅栏西街) and you will be assailed by the unique and pungent smell of stinky tofu. The food stalls that line the top of this *hutong* are a great place to sample Beijing street food. Try the pancake-like *jianbing, roubing,* bread filled with meat, or hold your nose and get an order of stinky tofu.

⑤ **Guanyin Temple**

Beijing's *hutong* are full of now-defunct little temples that were once the centre of the local community, some of which have been transformed into restaurants and homes. Dazhalan Xijie was originally called Guanyinsi Jie (观音寺街) after its temple, but all that remains of it is this plaque on a wall.

⑥ **Long Live the Revolution!**

There are precious few physical reminders of the Cultural Revolution left in Beijing, despite the fact that this incredibly turbulent period of Chinese history only ended in 1976. But look carefully at the **house** (27 Yingtao Xijie) here and you'll see the fading red characters for 'Long Live the Revolution' (革命万岁) daubed on the wall.

⑦ **Red Light Peking**

The maze of narrow lanes running off Dazhalan Xijie were notorious for being old Beijing's red light district. There are only a few reminders of this racy past left and one is the splendid-looking **Leo's Courtyard** (22 Shanxi Xiang 陕西巷胡同22号). It's now a backpacker hostel, but was formerly one of the most upmarket brothels in all Beijing.

ZHŌNGNÁNHĂI

Nánhăi Lake

Tiananmen West 天安门西 Ⓢ

Xichang'an Jie

Tian'anmen Square

Meishi Jie

Ⓧ 6 Meishi Jie

Ⓢ 5 National Centre for the Performing Arts (NCPA) Hepingmen Dongrongxian Hutong Beixinhua Jie 北新华街 Ⓢ Xironqxian Hutong 和平门

Qianmen Xiheyan Jie

Sanjing Hutong

Dazhalan Xijie

Zhushikou Xidajie 珠市口西大街

Beiwei Lu 北纬路 ✱ 13

Yong'an Lu

Hufang Lu

Fengfangliuli Jie

17 Ⓐ Liulichang Dongjie

Nanxinhua Jie

Tieshu Xie je

18 Ⓐ Liulichang Xijie

Xidan 西单

Naoshikou Zhongjie Xinwenhua Jie

Xuanwumen 宣武门

Xuanwumen Dajie

Ⓢ Xuanwumenwai Dajie 宣武门大街

Ⓢ Xuanwumen Xidajie

Shangxie Jie

Caishikou 菜市口 Ⓢ Caishikou Dajie

Mishi Hutong

Taipingqiao Dajie

Ⓢ Fuxingmen 复兴门

Circle Line

Changchunjie 长椿街

Xiaxie Jie

Changchun Jie

Guang'anmennei Dajie 广安门内大街

Jiaozi Hutong

Fayuan Temple 4 Ⓒ

Niu Jie

Nanheng Xijie

Nanlishilu Lu

Xibianmennei Dajie

Baiguang Lu

Guangyi Jie

Nanheng Xijie

Fuxingmenwai Dajie 复兴门内大街

Sanlihe Dong

1 Ⓒ Capital Museum

Nanlishilu 南礼士路 Ⓢ

White Cloud 3 Ⓒ Temple Baiyunguan Jie

Yinshan Qu

Lianhuachi Donglu

Baiyun Lu

To Beijing West Train Station (1.8km)

Hucheng River (City Moat)

Guang'anmen Nanbinhe Lu 安门大街北

Shoupakou Nanjie

Shoupakou Beijie

Guang'anmen Train Station 安门火车站 Ⓚ

Sights

Capital Museum

MUSEUM

1 Map p62, A5

The Capital Museum has raised the bar for every cultural institution in town, thanks to both its thoughtful presentation of some very impressive exhibits and the showcase building housing them. The galleries track the evolution of Beijing, as well as highlighting major Chinese cultural achievements. Be sure to visit the fascinating gallery devoted to Beijing folk customs. (首都博物馆; www.capital museum.org.cn; 16 Fuxingmenwai Dajie 复兴门外大街16号; admission free with passport; ⏰9am-5pm Tue-Sun; ⓢMuxidi)

Local Life
Houhai

Directly opposite the north gate of Beihai Park (p58), the three **Houhai lakes** (后海; ⓢShichahai, Nanluoguxiang or Jishuitan) are some of the capital's favourite outdoor spots. During the day, people fish, fly kites and in the summer swim (we wouldn't advise that). At night the many bars and restaurants here spring into life. The lakes are particularly good to cycle around and numerous places by the lakeshores hire out bikes by the hour (¥10 per hour, ¥200 deposit). In the winter, Houhai is the best place in the capital to ice-skate, and local vendors appear magically to rent you all the gear you'll need.

Miaoying Temple White Dagoba

BUDDHIST TEMPLE

2 Map p62, C3

The largest surviving Yuan dynasty (1206–1368) monument in Beijing, the chalk-white pagoda here looms large over the surrounding *hutong*, which are well worth meandering around as well. But the real highlights are the hundreds of glittering Tibetan Buddhist statues in the **Hall of the Great Enlightened One**. (妙应寺白塔; 171 Fuchengmennei Dajie 阜成门内大街171号; admission ¥20; ⏰9am-5pm Tue-Sun; ⓢXisi)

White Cloud Temple

TAOIST TEMPLE

3 Map p62, A6

Founded in AD 739, although most of the temple halls date from the Qing dynasty, this is a huge, lively and fascinating complex of shrines and courtyards, tended by Taoist monks with their hair gathered into topknots. Make sure to check out the **Hall of the Jade Emperor**, or join the housewives who cluster at the **Hall to the God of Wealth** to divine their financial future. (白云观; 9 Baiyunguan Jie 白云观街9号; adult ¥10; ⏰8.30am-4.30pm May-Oct, to 4pm Nov-Apr; ⓢMuxidi)

Fayuan Temple

BUDDHIST TEMPLE

4 Map p62, C8

Infused with an air of reverence and devotion, this lovely temple dates back originally to the 7th century. Now the **China Buddhism College**, it's always lively with worshippers and students. Don't miss the Guanyin Hall and its dishes. There's a tremendous selection of spring rolls for those who just want to graze while imbibing one of the excellent martinis (¥40), and live music some nights too. It's hidden down a *hutong* just off Gulou Xidajie. (肆角餐吧; 📞 6401 7797; www.these4corners .com; 27 Dashibei Hutong 大石碑胡同27号; dishes from ¥34; ⊙ 11am-3am; Ⓢ Shichahai; 😊 🛜 🖭)

Best Historic Hutong

Dashilar (p60)

Dazhalan Xijie (p60)

Shanxi Xiang (p60)

Ming dynasty-era statue of the goddess of mercy. (法源寺; 7 Fayuansi Qianjie; 法源寺前街7号; admission ¥5; ⊙ 8.30-5pm; Ⓢ Caishikou)

National Centre for the Performing Arts (NCPA)
CONCERT HALL

5 ◎ Map p62, E6

The cheeky locals call it the 'alien egg', but the dome-like NCPA looks more like the futuristic lair of a James Bond villain. It's now the premier spot in town to catch classical music, ballet and Western opera shows, but, love it or hate it, it's also one of the most eye-popping buildings in the capital. (国家大剧院; 2 Xichang'an Jie 西长安街 2号; admission ¥40; ⊙ 9am-5pm Tue-Sun; Ⓢ Tiananmen West)

Eating

4Corners
SOUTHEAST ASIAN $$

6 ✗ Map p62, E1

A laid-back spot with a cosy outside area, 4Corners serves up a medley of zingy Vietnamese and Thai-influenced

Yuelu Shanwu
CHINESE HUNAN $$

7 ✗ Map p62, E2

There's a marvellous view over Houhai (p64) here, while the catalogue-sized menu is heavy on the searing, spicy flavours of Hunan province. But not

Chinese New Year festival at White Cloud Temple

Diners at Goubuli

every dish will take the lining off your mouth; try the home-style pork or the boiled frog. (岳麓山屋; 📞6617 2696; 19a Qianhai Xiyan 什刹海前海西沿甲19号荷花市场内); dishes from ¥28; ⏰10.30am-1am; Ⓢ Shichahai orNanluoguxiang; 🏬)

Hutong Pizza
PIZZA $$

 Map p62, E2

Hard to find – it's down a *hutong* off Houhai – but make the effort because the trademark square, and very large, pizzas here are among the best in town. There are numerous options to choose from, or build your own. It has good veggie burgers, too. Book ahead at peak hours. (胡同比萨; 📞8322 8916; 9 Yindingqiao Hutong 什刹海银锭桥胡同9号院; pizzas from ¥65; ⏰11am-10.30pm; Ⓢ Shichahai; 🏬🏪)

Goubuli
CHINESE DUMPLINGS $

 Map p62, E7

Dumpling devotees will love this place. There are eight different types to pick from, including meat, prawn, crab and veggie options, as well as plenty of cold dishes to accompany them. Has a picture menu. (狗不理; 31 Dazhalan Jie 大栅栏街31号; dumplings from ¥12; ⏰7.30am-10pm; Ⓢ Qianmen)

Kong Yiji

CHINESE ZHEJIANG $$

10 Map p62, D1

Some of the dishes here – such as 'drunken' shrimp (醉虾; *zuixia*) – come swimming in the sherry-like wine Zhejiang is famous for. Also popular at this big and bustling place are the many alcohol-free pork and fish dishes, such as the very addictive *dongporou* (东坡肉). There's no English menu; take a look at what other people are eating and point. (孔乙己酒店; ☎6618 4915; Deshengmennei Dajie, Shichahai, Houhai Nan'an 德胜门内大街什刹海后海南岸; dishes from ¥28; ⏰11am-10pm; S Jishuitan)

Le Petit Saigon

FRENCH, VIETNAMESE $$

11 Map p62, E1

Cool, stylish bistro with a menu that mixes classic Vietnamese, such as *pho* and lemon chicken, and French dishes, such as beef bourguignon, to decent effect. The desserts are especially good. There's a strong wine list and proper coffee, which you can enjoy on the roof terrace in the summer. (西贡在巴黎; ☎6401 8465; 141 Jiugulou Dajie 旧鼓楼大街141号; mains from ¥58; ⏰10.30am-11pm; S Shichahai; 📶 🗐)

Drinking

Bed Bar

BAR

12 Map p62, E1

A wicked layout of interconnected rooms and traditional Chinese beds make Bed a great spot; even if it's crowded there's normally somewhere to hide away if you want. There are DJs at the weekend and proper mixed drinks, too. There's a sign at the entrance of the alley to guide you here. (床吧; 17 Zhangwang Hutong, Jiugulou Dajie 旧鼓楼大街张旺胡同17号; beers/cocktails from ¥25/40; S Gulou Dajie)

> Top Tip
>
> **Hidden Houhai**
>
> Come nightfall, the Houhai lakes area becomes a throng of milling crowds and bar touts trying to entice you into their pricey hostelries. Avoid both by slipping down the *hutong* that run off the lakeshore, where you'll find far more amenable bars and cafes. The lanes running west from Silver Ingot Bridge, at the end of Yandai Xiejie, and the west shore of Qianhai Lake are a good place to start.

Entertainment

Tianqiao Acrobatics Theatre

ACROBATICS

13 Map p62, E8

West of the Temple of Heaven Park (p50), this 100-year-old theatre offers one of Beijing's best acrobatic displays, a one-hour show performed by the Beijing Acrobatic Troupe. It's less touristy than the other venues, and the high-wire display here is thrilling. The entrance is down the eastern side of the building. (天桥杂技剧场; ☑6303 7449; 95 Tianqiao Shichang Jie 天桥市场街95号; tickets ¥180-380; ⊗performances 5.30pm; Ⓢ Taoranting or Caishikou)

Huguang Guild Hall

PEKING OPERA

14 ⭐ Map p62, D8

With its magnificent red, green and gold interior, the historic Huguang (built in 1807) is a great place to experience your first Peking opera. There's a small **opera museum** (¥10; ⊗9am-5pm) opposite the theatre. (湖广会馆; ☑6351 8284; 3 Hufang Lu 虎坊路3号; tickets ¥180-680; ⊗performances 6.30pm; Ⓢ Caishikou)

East Shore Jazz Café

JAZZ

15 ⭐ Map p62, E2

This chilled venue is the place to hear the best local jazz bands. There are live performances from Wednesday to Sunday (from 10pm), in a comfortable, welcoming atmosphere. There's a small roof terrace open in summer with a nice view of Houhai (p64). No cover charge, but it's worth booking a table here on weekends when it gets busy. (东岸; ☑8403 2131; 2nd fl, 2 Shichahai Nanyan 什刹海南沿2号楼2层; beers/cocktails from ¥35/40; ⊗3pm-2am; Ⓢ Shichahai)

Shops in a Xicheng *hutong*

Shopping

Three Stone Kite Shop
KITES

16 🔒 Map p62, E2

Kites by appointment to the former Qing emperors; the great-grandfather of the owner of this friendly store used to make the kites for the Chinese royal family. There's a tremendous selection in all sizes here, as well as miniature framed kites, which make great gifts. (三石斋风筝; 25 Di'anmen Xi-dajie 地安门西大街甲25号; ⊙ 9am-9pm; S Shichahai or Nanluoguxiang)

Yuehaixuan Musical Instrument Store
MUSICAL INSTRUMENTS

17 🔒 Map p62, D7

Fantastic, friendly emporium that specialises in traditional Chinese musical instruments, such as the zither-like *guzheng,* the *erhu* and *banhu* (two-string Chinese violins), and *gu* (drums). It does great gongs and has many esoteric instruments from Tibet and Mongolia as well. (乐海轩门市部; 97 Liulichang Dongjie 琉璃厂东街97号; ⊙9.30am-6pm; S Hepingmen)

Rongbaozhai
CHINESE ART

18 🔒 Map p62, D7

Calligraphy, scroll paintings, wood-block prints, paper, ink and brushes are on offer at this state-run establishment, which sprawls down the road. Prices are supposedly fixed, but you can often get 10% off. (荣宝斋; 19

Maliandao Tea Market

The largest tea market in northern China, **Maliandao** (马连道茶城; 6 Maliandao Lu 马连道路6号; ⊙9am-7pm; S Beijing West Station) is a great place to investigate the Chinese passion for tea. The vendors here are normally happy to let you sample their brews, while Maliandao Lu itself has hundreds of tea shops, where prices for tea and tea sets are lower than in tourist areas. The market is located about 1.5km south of the Beijing West station.

Liulichang Xijie 琉璃厂西街19号; ⊙9am-5.30pm; S Hepingmen)

Ruifuxiang Silk
CHINESE CLOTHING

19 🔒 Map p62, E2

A newish branch of one of China's most famous brands; come here for all manner of quality silk items, from scarves and shawls to slippers and hats. It's a great place to pick up a traditional Chinese dress *(qipao),* as well as cute kids outfits. (瑞蚨祥; 50 Di'anmenwai Dajie; Dongdajie 地安门外大街50号; ⊙10am-8.30pm; S Shichahai)

Explore

North Chaoyang

Home to Sanlitun (三里屯), Beijing's principal nightlife hub, north Chaoyang has bars and clubs aplenty, as well as a staggering selection of restaurants, including both fine dining options and local eateries. But north Chaoyang (朝阳北) isn't just about epicurean pleasures and hedonism. Head to the 798 Art District to see why the Chinese contemporary art scene is the most exciting in the world.

The Sights in a Day

 North Chaoyang is the least sight-heavy district in all Beijing. But before you devote yourself to pleasure, make sure to pop into the **Dongyue Temple** (p77) to visit its cast of demons. It's the capital's most morbid shrine, and one of its most memorable. Once you're done, it's a short trip to the **Sanlitun Yashow Clothing Market** (p83), where you can test your haggling skills.

 You're spoiled for lunch venues in this part of town, but we like **Bocata** (p78) for its Mediterranean/Middle Eastern eats, as well as the MSG-free Cantonese cuisine at **Herbal Café** (p79). Then jump on a bus or take a taxi ride north to the **798 Art District** (p72) to spend the afternoon gallery-hopping.

🌙 Get dressed up for a night of revelry. If you're feeling flush, **Duck de Chine** (p78) has an artful blend of French and Chinese duck dishes, or there's the Asian fusion cuisine at **Bei** (p78). Afterwards, it's time for cocktails. **Apothecary** (p79) is home to some of the capital's best mixologists, or there's the roof terrace at **Migas** (p79) to lounge on. Still not ready for bed? Then head to one of the nearby clubs and throw some shapes.

For a local's night out in Sanlitun, see p74

👁 Top Sights
798 Art District (p72)

🔍 Local Life
Sip Cocktails in Sanlitun (p74)

❤ Best of Beijing

Best Food
Bei (p78)

Duck de Chine (p78)

Herbal Café (p79)

Best Drinking
Apothecary (p79)

George's (p75)

Migas (p79)

Glen (p75)

Best Markets
Sanlitun Yashow Clothing Market (p83)

Getting There

S **Subway** For Sanlitun, take Line 2 to Dongsi Shitiao or Line 10 to Tuanjiehu. To get to the Dongyue Temple, use Line 2 and get off at Chaoyangmen.

🚌 **Bus** Bus 909 (¥2) runs from exit C of the Dongzhimen subway station to the 798 Art District.

Top Sights
798 Art District 大山子艺术区

The 798 Art District *(Qi Jiu Ba Yishu Qu)*, also known as Dashanzi (大山子), is where the Chinese contemporary art boom began. Housed in a vast and sprawling former electronics factory, its numerous galleries remain the centre of the Beijing art scene. The area has also sprouted cafes and restaurants, and you can easily spend a day here exploring the galleries while musing on how the factory's transformation into a global art hub mirrors China's march from Maoism to capitalism.

👁 off Map p76

Jiuxianqiao Lu; 酒仙桥路

Admission free, but some exhibitions require tickets

🕑 galleries 10am-6pm, some closed Mon

🚍 909

Communist slogans on gallery walls

Don't Miss

BTAP

BTAP (Ceramics Third St; ☻10am-6pm Tue-Sun), or Beijing Tokyo Arts Projects, was one of the original 798 galleries and, as the name suggests, showcases not just Chinese artists, but Japanese (and sometimes Korean) ones, too. As with many of the galleries in 798, multimedia and installations are big here; they're ideally suited to the huge space this gallery occupies.

UCCA

As much an arts centre as it is a gallery, **UCCA** (798 Rd; admission ¥10, free Thu;☻10am-7pm Tue-Sun) has four exhibition spaces spread over a vast 8000 sq metres in a Bauhaus-inspired setting. As well as showing some of the best Chinese artists, it holds film screenings, workshops, educational programs and mini festivals, and also has a funky shop selling designer products.

Galleria Continua

Located just below a towering brick chimney, **Galleria Continua** (just south of 797 Rd; ☻11am-6pm Tue-Sun) is another long-standing gallery and it exhibits both Chinese and foreign artists, including some very big names. Smaller than some of the other spaces in 798, it's still one of the most visually arresting of all the galleries here.

PACE

The Beijing outpost of a famed New York gallery, **PACE** (797 Rd; ☻11am-7pm Tue-Sun) represents some of the most acclaimed Chinese artists, including Yue Minjun and native Beijinger Li Songsong. It's another monster space and amazing to view art in.

☑ Top Tips

▸ Many of the galleries are closed on Mondays, so plan ahead.

▸ Keep an eye out for the communist slogans daubed on the walls of some galleries; a reminder of 798's past as a model factory built in the 1950s.

▸ Dedicated art fans should also check out Caochangdi (草场地), another colony of galleries 3km north of 798.

✕ Take a Break

The **At Café** (798 Rd; ☻10am-11pm; 🛜📱) was the original hipster hangout in 798 – check out the artfully designed holes in the interior walls – and remains a popular spot for coffee and Western comfort food. **Timezone 8** (798 Rd; ☻8.30am-8pm; 🛜📱) is a great cafe that does everything from burgers to sushi. It's attached to the equally excellent bookshop of the same name, which specialises, unsurprisingly, in art, architecture and design titles.

Local Life
Sip Cocktails in Sanlitun

A few years ago, Sanlitun (三里屯) was very much an area for expats and visiting foreigners. How times have changed. Now, there are more locals hitting the bars and clubs that cluster here than ever before, making this a real melting pot of an area and a good place to meet young Beijingers out on the razz.

❶ Backstreet Bars

Dive into the little passageways to the side of **Sanlitun Village** (p83), where hidden hostelries are tucked away on tiny streets or in courtyards. Good spots to start the night off are at **The Tree** (树酒吧; 43 Sanlitun Beijie 三里屯北街43号; beers from ¥15; ☺11am-late Mon-Sat, 1pm-late Sun; Ⓢ Tuanjiehu), which also serves wicked pizzas, and **First Floor** (壹楼; ground fl, Tongli Studios, Sanlitun Houjie 三里屯后街同里1层; beer from ¥15,

cocktails from ¥35, ⏱10am-2am; Ⓢ Tuanjiehu), which has an unpretentious, pub-like vibe.

❷ Beautiful People

Mesh (bldg 1, Village, 11 Sanlitun Lu 三里屯路11号院1号楼; cocktails from ¥70; ⏱5pm-1am; Ⓢ Tuanjiehu) has been designed to within an inch of its life – white bar, mirrors, fancy light fittings and mesh screens separating its different areas – and so have many of the clientele. But it's still fun and the lychee martinis are justly popular. On Thursday, it's gay-friendly.

❸ Shaved Ice Cubes

Beijing has a number of very discreet Japanese-themed bars that serve some of the finest drinks in town. Once inside **Glen** (2nd fl, 203 Taiyue Haoting, 16 Nansanlitun Lu 南三里路16号泰悦豪庭2层203; cocktails from ¥80; ⏱6pm-2am; Ⓢ Tuanjiehu; 🛜), you enter a world where the barman wears a dinner jacket and will serve you a perfect mixed drink, or a rare single malt whisky complete with an ice cube that has been shaved into the shape of a ball.

❹ George's

There's a growing selection of high-quality bars hidden beneath the stands of the Workers Stadium itself.

George's (near gate 12, east side of Workers Stadium, Gongrentiyuchang Donglu 工人体育场东路; 工人体育场东门内12号入口; cocktails from ¥70; ⏱3pm-2am; Ⓢ Tuanjiehu) is perhaps the best: a thoughtfully designed spot with an extensive cocktail list that's fine for an earlier quiet drink, or good with a crowd later on.

❺ Vics & Mix

At the north gate of the Workers Stadium, the bars give way to some of Beijing's longest-running clubs. Neither **Vics** (威克斯; Fri & Sat ¥50; ⏱7pm-late; Ⓢ Dongsishitiao) nor **Mix** (密克斯; admission ¥50; ⏱8pm-late; Ⓢ Dongsi Shitiao) are the most sophisticated nightclubs in the world, but they pump out a similar soundtrack of party hip-hop and R&B and are consistently busy. Solo travellers: if you can't score here, you never will.

❻ Cargo

If house and techno are more your thing, then try **Cargo** (6 Gongrentiyuchang Xilu; 工人体育场西路6号; admission ¥50; ⏱8pm-late; Ⓢ Chaoyangmen), which flies in big-name international DJs and caters to an enthusiastic locals-dominated crowd. It's on a strip of dance clubs, so you can club-hop here if you wish.

500 m
0.25 miles

Chaoyang Park

Maizidian Jie

798 Art District

Agricultural Exhibition Center (Nongye Zhanlanguan)
农业展览馆

Agricultural Exhibition Center

Nongzhanguan Nanlu 农展馆南路

Tuanjiehu
团结湖

Tuanjiehu Lu

Tuanjiechu Park

Hujialou
呼家楼

Hujialou Beije

Dongsanhuan Beilu (East 3rd Ring Rd) 东三环北路

SÀNLÌTÚN EMBASSY AREA

Sanlitun Lu

Sanlitun Xilujie

Sanlitun Xiwujie

Sanlitun Dongsijie

Sanlitun Dong'erjie

Sanlitun Beije

Sanlitun Beije

Yaojiayuan Lu

Baijiazhuang Lu

Nansanlitun Lu

Chaoyang Beilu

Chaoyang Dajie

Chaoyang Beilu

Dongzhimenwai Xiaojie

Dongzhimenwai Dajie 东直门外大街

CHÁOYÁNG

Chunxiu Lu

Xingfucun Lu

Bodhi Therapeutic Retreat

Gongrentiyuchang Beilu 工人体育场北路

Xindong Lu

Gongrentiyuchang Donglu 工人体育场东路

Workers Stadium

Gongrentiyuchang Nanlu

Gongtentiyuchang Xilu

JIÀNGUÓMÉNWÀI EMBASSY AREA

Dongdaqiao Lu

Chaoyangmenwai Dajie 朝阳门外大街

Dongyue Temple 东岳庙

Chaoyangmenwai Dajie

Chaoyangmen
朝阳门

Dongzhimen
东直门

Dongzhimen Beidajie 东直门北大街

Dongzhong Jie

Xinzhong Lu

Workers Gymnasium

Dongsi Shitiao

Dongsi Shitiao

Dongzhong Jie

Chaoyangmen Beidajie 朝阳门北大街

Chaoyangmen Beidajie

1

2

3

4

A B C D E

Sights

Dongyue Temple

TAOIST TEMPLE

1 ◉ Map p76, B4

Beijing's most morbid temple, Dongyue is populated by hundreds of life-sized ghoul and ghost statues, who offer protection from harassment in the netherworld in return for devotion and a suitable offering. Still a working Taoist temple, Dongyue is dedicated to the god of Taishan (one of China's five holy mountains). (东岳庙; 141 Chaoyangmenwai Dajie 朝阳门外大街141号; admission ¥10; ⏰8.30am-4.30pm Tue-Sun; Ⓢ Chaoyangmen)

Bodhi Therapeutic Retreat

MASSAGE

2 ◉ Map p76, B2

This serene and upscale spa is the perfect place to rejuvenate after a hard day pounding Beijing's streets. There are great Chinese and Thai massages, as well as wraps and facials. The foot reflexology massages are especially good. There are 20% discounts before 5pm during the week. It's opposite the north gate of the Workers Stadium. (菩提会所; 17 Gongrentiyuchang Beilu 工人体育场北路17号; massages from ¥168; ⏰11am-midnight; Ⓢ Dongsi Shitiao)

Performers at Dongyue Temple

RICHARD I'ANSON/GETTY IMAGES ©

Eating

Bei
NORTH ASIAN $$$

3 Map p76, C2

Very hip restaurant that fuses the cuisine of Korea, Japan and northern China to great effect. The sushi and sashimi (flown in daily from Tokyo) is top-notch, the tuna outstanding, and there's a strong selection of *saki* and *soju* to keep you in high spirits. Reserve ahead here. (北; ☎6410 5230; The Opposite House, Bld 1, 11 Sanlitun Lu 三里屯路11号院1号楼; mains ¥150-400; ◷6-10pm; ⑤Tuanjiehu; 🅟)

Duck de Chine
FRENCH/CHINESE DUCK $$$

4 Map p76, C3

Housed in a reconstructed industrial-style courtyard complex known as 1949, this chic restaurant incorporates both Chinese and French duck-roasting methods to produce some stand-out duck dishes, including a leaner version of the classic Peking duck (¥238). It has an excellent wine list. Book ahead. (全鸭季; ☎6501 8881; Courtyard 4, 1949, off Gongrentiyuchang Beilu 工人体育场北路4号院1949内; mains ¥50-150; ◷11am-2pm & 5.30-10pm; ⑤Tuanjiehu; 🅟)

Baoyuan Dumpling Restaurant
CHINESE DUMPLINGS $

5 Map p76, D1

Fun for the kids – but delicious for parents as well – this restaurant dazzles diners with its multicoloured *jiaozi* (饺子; boiled dumplings). The dough dyes are all natural (carrots for orange, spinach for green) and the fillings are as good as you'll find in Beijing. (宝源饺子屋; 6 Maizidian Jie 麦子店街6号; mains ¥20-40, dumplings ¥10-16; ◷11.15am-10pm; ⑤Liangmaqiao or Agricultural Exhibition Centre; 🅟)

Bocata
CAFE $

6 Map p76, C2

Great spot for coffee or lunch, especially in the summer when the outdoor terrace gets crowded. There's a vague Mediterranean and Middle Eastern theme to the food: falafels and decent hummus, as well as solid salads and tasty sandwiches on ciabatta. Has top-class chips, too. (☎6417 5291; 3 Sanlitun Beilu 三里屯北路3号; sandwiches ¥26-50; ◷11.30am-midnight; ⑤Tuanjiehu; 🛜)

Purple Haze
THAI $$

7 Map p76, B2

Beijing's trendiest Thai, with a reliable take on classics such as tom yum soup and red and green curries. The tangy, spicy salads are especially good. But the purple decor takes a bit of getting used to. It's down an alley with a branch of the ICBC bank at the top. (紫苏庭; ☎6413 0899; 55 Xingfu Yicun, off Gongrentiyuchang Beilu; 工人体育场北路幸福一村55号; mains ¥40-70; ◷11.30am-10.30pm; ⑤Dongsi Shitiao; 😋)

Local Life

Shopping Mall Restaurants

In Beijing, shopping malls are often home to some excellent restaurants and **Sanlitun Village** (p83) has a number of fine spots to graze in. The smoke-free **Herbal Café** (泰和草本工坊; ☎6416 0618; 3rd fl, Village, 19 Sanlitun Lu 三里屯路19号Village 3层; soups from ¥20; ☉11am-11pm; ⓢTuanjiehu; ♿ 🎘) is great for cheap Hong Kong–style eats, including dim sum and tasty soups (which come in cool canisters). Also very popular is **Element Fresh**, (北京新元素餐厅; ☎6417 1318; 3rd fl, Village, 19 Sanlitun Lu 三里屯路19号Village 3层; sandwiches & salads from ¥58; ☉11am-11pm Mon-Fri, 8am-11pm Sat & Sun; ⓢTuanjiehu; ♿ 🎘), which offers a mix of healthy and hefty salads, sandwiches and MSG-free mains.

Xinjiang Red Rose Restaurant
CHINESE XINJIANG $

8 🍴 Map p76, B2

Specialising in the Central Asian–style cuisine of China's far west; eating here is like hanging out at a raucous party. Communal seating is at long canteen-style tables, and when the Uighur music and dancers get going (from 7pm) it's very loud. It does good lamb skewers (¥10). It's down an alley opposite the north gate of the Workers' Stadium. (新疆红玫瑰餐厅; ☎6415 5741;

7 Xingfu Yicun, off Gongrentiyuchang Beilu, 工人体育场北路幸福一村7号; dishes from ¥15; ☉11am-11pm; ⓢDongsi Shitiao)

Drinking

Apothecary
BAR

9 🍷 Map p76, C2

With its lovingly prepared cocktails (the menu includes a brief history of the classic drinks) and some very impressive bar snacks, Apothecary has become the cocktail bar of choice for many in Beijing. It's much more relaxed than its swanky, 5-star hotel competitors but the service can be slow and there's a bizarre no-standing policy. (酒术; 3rd fl Nali Patio, 81 Sanlitun Beilu 三里屯北路81号那里花园3层; cocktails from ¥60; ☉6pm-late Tue-Sun; ⓢTuanjiehu)

Migas
BAR

A bar and Spanish restaurant, Migas becomes wildly popular in the summer when its rooftop terrace – the highest and arguably the coolest spot in Sanlitun's Nali Patio (see 9 🍷 Map p76; C2) – comes into its own. The food isn't as good as the drinks (there's an excellent wine list), although the tapas has its fans; instead it's the city views and laid-back but hip atmosphere that makes Migas a winner. (米家思; 6th fl Nali Patio, 81 Sanlitun Beilu 三里屯北路81号那里花园6层; beer/cocktails from ¥25/50; ☉noon-2.30pm & 6-10.30pm, bar 7.30pm-late; ⓢTuanjiehu)

Q Bar
BAR

10 Map p76, C3

One of Beijing's longer-standing bars, and one of the first to become popular with both locals and foreigners, Q Bar remains a very amenable spot in which to sample a libation or three. In the summer, there's a useful roof terrace to decamp to. Look for the big 'Q' hanging off the side of the Eastern Inn Hotel to guide you there. (Q吧; 6th fl, Eastern Inn Hotel, Nansanlitun Lu 南三里屯路; cocktails from ¥50; ⏰6pm-late; Ⓢ Tuanjiehu)

Bookworm
CAFE

11 Map p76, C3

A combination of cafe, bar and lending library, the Bookworm is now a

Beijing institution. It's the place to hear visiting authors talk, hunker down over the laptop, browse the huge library or kick back over coffee, cocktails and food. The annual literary festival organised by Bookworm every March is one of Beijing's premier cultural events. Head to the roof terrace in the summer. (书虫; www .beijingbookworm.com; Bldg 4, Nansanlitun Lu 南三里屯路4号楼; coffee from ¥25, beers from ¥20; ⏰9am-2am; Ⓢ Tuanjiehu; ⊖ 🛜)

d Lounge
BAR

12 Map p76, C3

High ceilings and exposed brick walls give this cool venue the feel of a converted factory. The bright white bar adds some futuristic flavour, while the drinks are well made (although some complain of slightly obnoxious staff). Popular, but hard to find; look for the lower-case 'd'. (Courytard 4, Gongrentiyuchang Beilu 工人体育场北路4号院; cocktails from ¥50; ⏰7pm-late; Ⓢ Tuanjiehu)

Destination
CLUB

13 Map p76, B3

This grey concrete block might not look enticing, and the interior decor isn't much better, but as Beijing's only genuine gay club it's jammed every weekend with boys who like boys and girls who want a break from them. (目的地; 7 Gongrentiyuchang Xilu 工人体育场西路7号; admission ¥60; ⏰8pm-late; Ⓢ Chaoyangmen)

Local Life

Karaoke

Karaoke bars (known as 'KTV') are where Beijingers go to unwind after work and to celebrate. Once you get over being shy of singing in public (alcohol helps), karaoke is a lot of fun. The best way to try it is with some locals; otherwise head to **Melody** (麦乐迪; A-77 Chaoyangmenwai Dajie 朝阳门外大街A-77号; r per hr ¥179-229; ⏰10am-2am; Ⓢ Chaoyangmen) or **Partyworld** (钱柜; Fanli Bldg, 22 Chaoyangmenwai Dajie 朝阳门外大街22号泛利大厦; small r per hr ¥200-260; ⏰noon-6am; Ⓢ Chaoyangmen), both of which have a selection of English-language tunes as well as snacks and drinks.

Top Tip
Seedy Sanlitun

These days, the main drag of San-litun Lu is rather tawdry – at night the touts for massage parlours and hookers emerge – and the bars are strictly for the undiscerning. Don't let the people lurking outside them drag you in; the drinks are expensive and/or fake and there are far better places in which to imbibe nearby.

World of Suzie Wong CLUB

 14 🔘 Map p76, E2

Still jumping most nights, Suzie Wong's opium-den chic with a 21st-century twist has made it a Beijing nightlife legend. The dance floor, roof terrace and traditional Chinese-style beds you can lounge on, plus some decent sounds, attract a very mixed crowd, from models to business types and working girls. The entrance is just by the west gate of Chaoyang Park. (苏西黄; 1a Nongzhanguan Nanlu 农展馆南路甲1号; admission ¥50 Wed-Sat, women free; ⏱7pm-late; S Tuanjiehu)

Entertainment

Universal Theatre (Heaven & Earth Theatre) ACROBATICS

15 ⭐ Map p76, A2

Young performers from the China National Acrobatic Troupe perform their eye- and joint-popping contortions. It's a favourite with tour groups, so try to book ahead. Tickets are pricier the further from the stage you sit. Keep an eye out for the dismal white tower that looks like it should be in an airport – that's where you buy your tickets. (天地剧场; 10 Dongzhimen Nanda-jie 东直门南大街10号; tickets ¥180-680; ⏱performance 7.15pm; S Dongsi Shitiao)

Chaoyang Theatre ACROBATICS, PEKING OPERA

16 ⭐ Map p76, D4

Hosts splendid daily performances by visiting acrobatics troupes from all over China, as well as Peking opera

LOU LINWEI/ALAMY ©

World of Suzie Wong

Understand

Modern Life in Beijing

Walk around Sanlitun with its hordes of trendy, twenty-something locals and you could be forgiven for thinking that China was never a country in the grip of Maoist ideology. But as recently as the 1980s, a luxury item in China meant a bicycle or radio, not the latest model iPhone, while food rationing didn't stop until 1993.

These days, though, it is no exaggeration to say that life has never been better for Beijingers. The capital's residents have always been convinced that they live at the centre of the world and now, as China ascends to genuine superpower status, it seems that they really do. For young people in particular, the combination of rising incomes and greater access to education means they are enjoying a freedom that was unthinkable for their parents.

Material Dreams

The goal of a better life is the aspiration of every local. The new buildings and shopping malls that line the centre of Beijing are twin temples to the gods of money and status that many people worship. Owning an apartment and a car is considered essential, even as the price of property in Beijing has accelerated far beyond the means of many. Politics is barely mentioned, at least not in public, and as Beijingers flock to buy the cars that are the principal reason for the poor air quality in the capital, environmental issues are still low on the local agenda. More than anything, the huge and rapid changes the capital has undergone in recent years mean that people tend to look forward, rather than dwelling on the often unpleasant past.

Family First

Even though life for many in Beijing seems unrecognisable from what it was even at the turn of the millenium, its core tenets remain the same. The family is still the very heart of society, and three generations often live together under one cramped roof. And while their children work and grandchildren study, it is the elderly more than anyone who do as Beijingers have always done, hanging out in the *hutong* or streets chatting, playing Chinese chess and mah jong and roaming the city's parks.

shows sometimes. Many hotels can book tickets for here. (朝阳剧场; 36 Dongsanhuan Beilu 东三环北路36号; tickets ¥180-880; ⊘performances 5.15pm & 7.15pm; Ⓢ Hujialou)

Shopping

Sanlitun Village SHOPPING MALL

 Map p76, C2

This ultramodern, eye-catching collection of midsized malls is both a shopping and architectural highlight. The complex is in two sections. The **South Village** is home to the world's largest Adidas shop and a number of midrange Western clothing stores. The newer **North Village** is home to more high-end labels and local designer boutiques, including Emporio Armani, Comme des Garcons and Shanghai Trio. (19 Sanlitun Lu 三里屯路19号; ⊘10am-10pm; Ⓢ Tuanjiehu)

Sanlitun Yashow Clothing Market
CLOTHING, MARKET

18 🔒 Map p76, C2

A favourite with expats and visitors, this has five floors of virtually anything you might need. Basement: shoes, handbags and suitcases. First floor: coats and jackets. Second floor: shirts, suits and ladies wear. Third floor: silk, clothes, carpets, fabrics and tailors to fashion your raw material into something wearable. Fourth floor: jewellery, souvenirs, toys and a beauty salon. Bargain hard here. (三里屯雅秀服装市场; 58 Gongrentiyuchang Beilu 工人体育场北路58号; ⊘10am-9pm; Ⓢ Tuanjiehu)

Bainaohui COMPUTERS & ELECTRONICS

19 🔒 Map p76, B4

Four floors of gadgetry, including computers, mp3 players, blank CDs and DVDs, gaming gear, software and other accessories. The prices are fairly competitive and you can haggle, but don't expect too much of a reduction. Next to this mall there are a number of shops where you can pick up mobile phones and local SIM cards. (百脑汇电脑市场; 10 Chaoyangmenwai Dajie 朝阳门外大街10号; ⊘9am-8pm; Ⓢ Chaoyangmen or Hujialou)

Explore

South Chaoyang

South Chaoyang (朝阳南) has undergone the mother of all make-overs in recent years. Dominated by the spectacular CCTV building, the new skyscrapers of the central business district (CBD) abound with fashionable eateries and bars. Shopaholics will be in heaven here, as there are markets and malls galore, as well as the outlets of the leading local designers. Get ready to bargain hard.

The Sights in a Day

☀ If it's the weekend, you just have to force yourself out of bed early to get to the **Panjiayuan Antique Market** (p86), where you can go in search of hidden treasures. You could easily spend the whole morning here, and leave with your arms full.

☀ Grab lunch at **Najia Xiaoguan** (p91), an old Beijing standby in this part of town. From here, make a quick diversion to gaze in awe at the nearby **CCTV Building** (p91), the most eye-catching of all the new buildings that have sprung up in the capital. Then it's time for more shopping. The markets and malls in the area are an essential stop, but try to make time to visit some of the more offbeat shops here.

☽ Shopping done, there are some excellent dining options. **Din Tai Fung** (p91) has some of the most superb dumplings you'll find anywhere, or there's fine Western dining at **Grill 79** (p93). Finish the evening with a drink at **Atmosphere** (p93), Beijing's loftiest bar, or hit **Haze** (p92), home of Beijing's best DJ's.

For a local's day in South Chaoyang, see p88

👁 Top Sights
Panjiayuan Antique Market (p86)

◯ Local Life
Shop Like a Beijinger (p88)

🖤 Best of Beijing

Best Food
Najia Xiaoguan (p91)

Din Tai Fung (p91)

Grill 79 (p93)

Best Drinking & Nightlife
Atmosphere (p93)

Haze (p92)

Stone Boat (p91)

Best Markets
Panjiayuan Antique Market (p86)

Silk Market (p88)

Beijing Curio City (p93)

Getting There

S Subway Line 10 cuts north–south through South Chaoyang, while the venerable Line 1 runs east–west across it. Take Line 10 to Jinsong for the Panjiayuan Antique Market. For the CCTV building, use the Jintaixizhao stop on Line 10. Get off at Jianguomen and Yong'anli on Line 1 for Ritan Park and the Silk Market, respectively.

Top Sights
Panjiayuan Antique Market

By far the best place in Beijing to shop for arts, crafts and antiques is this wonderfully chaotic market (潘家园古玩市场; *Panjiayuan Guwan Shichang*). With around 3000 dealers here, what's on view is nothing less than a compendium of Chinese curios and an A to Z of Middle Kingdom knick-knacks. It's at its biggest and best on the weekends, when up to 50,000 visitors a day descend on it in search of that rare piece of Ming dynasty porcelain that will change their lives.

◎ Map p90, C5

West of Panjiayuan Bridge: 潘家园桥西侧

🕓 8.30am-6pm Mon-Fri, 4.30am-6pm Sat & Sun

Ⓢ Jinsong

Market vendors at Panjiayuan Antique Market

Don't Miss

Carpets
Panjiayuan is an excellent spot to pick up a new rug. There's a wide selection of carpets, both old and new, from all over China: from Xinjiang, in the far west, to Tibet. Antique carpets are often the best buy: they are handmade and have rich colours from the use of natural dyes.

Communist Kitsch
Mao memorabilia remains one of Beijing's most popular souvenirs and this is the best place to pick some up. Mao's *Little Red Book,* a collection of his quotations, is still the number-one seller. But if that doesn't do it for you, you can find Mao watches and 1970s-era alarm clocks, or lighters emblazoned with the Great Helmsman's image that play the Chinese national anthem.

Paintings & Posters
There's an awful lot of calligraphy on offer here, along with ink scroll paintings of Chinese landscapes. Be discerning, though, because much of it is not particularly memorable or valuable. One good buy is old Shanghai cigarette posters from the 1920s and '30s. They will increase in value, but make sure you are buying an original.

Garage Sales
Panjiayuan started life in the early 1980s as a place where locals could sell all the stuff they and their families had been hoarding during the years when free enterprise was not allowed. On the fringes of the market, you'll still find people selling what seems to be the contents of their attics. Browse carefully, and you might find a few gems.

☑ Top Tips

▶ While the market runs every day, it's much more fun at weekends.

▶ The early bird catches the worm here. On weekends especially, the earlier you get here the more chance you will have of finding something valuable and you won't be fighting your way through the crowds.

▶ Normal Beijing bargaining rules (pay half of the price asked) don't apply here. Some vendors will start at 10 times the price. Bargain hard and be sure to compare prices.

✖ Take a Break

There are numerous food stalls and hole-in-the-wall restaurants scattered throughout the market and surrounding it; choose one that's busy and you can't go wrong. Otherwise, head back north by metro to **Din Tai Fung** (p91), which serves wonderful dumplings in a clean and fresh environment.

Local Life
Shop Like a Beijinger

Shopping is the principal hobby of the locals. For a Beijinger, there's nothing better than a bargain, or the prospect of finding one, and the malls and markets in South Chaoyang are packed at all hours. They're the perfect places to learn how to shop like a Beijinger and to discover just how shopping savvy you really are.

1 Silk Market 秀水市场

A Beijing legend, the **Silk Market** (14 Dongdaqiao Lu 东大桥路14号; ⊘10am-8.30pm; **S** Yong'anli) is the perfect place to get into haggling mode. Staffed by a cunning crew of young women who will alternately flatter and cajole you into purchasing their wares at inflated prices, the market is known for its high-quality clothing fakes, but the silk is genuine and it's also a good place to find cashmere.

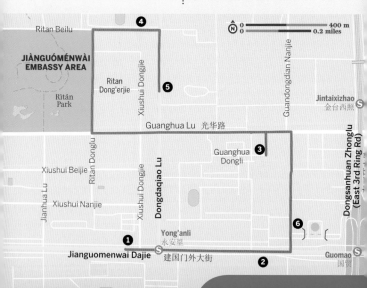

Ritan Beilu

JIÀNGUÓMÉNWÀI EMBASSY AREA

Ritán Park

Ritan Dong'erjie

Xiushui Dongjie

Guandongdian Nanjie

4

5

Jintaixizhao 金台西照 **S**

Guanghua Lu 光华路

Xiushui Beijie

Ritan Dongilu

Xiushui Dongjie

Dongdaqiao Lu

Guanghua Dongli

3

Dongsanhuan Zhonglu (East 3rd Ring Rd)

Jianhua Lu

Xiushui Nanjie

6

Yong'anli 永安里 **S**

1

Jianguomenwai Dajie 建国门外大街

2

Guomao 国贸 **S**

N 0 ——————— 400 m
0 ——————— 0.2 miles

② **Five Colours Earth** 五色土

There's a growing number of quality, home-grown fashion designers in Beijing. The women behind **Five Colours Earth** (25th fl, Bldg 14, Jianwai Soho, 39 Dongsanhuan Zhonglu 东三环中路 39号建外Soho14楼25层; ⏱10am-5pm; ⑤Guomao) do hip tops, skirts and jackets with a traditional Chinese twist. The clothes all incorporate the elaborate embroidery unique to the Miao ethnic minority in southwest China. Most of their gear is sold abroad; you can pick it up far cheaper here.

③ **Xiao Wang's Family Restaurant** 小王府

Take a lunch break at this old Beijing favourite. **Xiao Wang's** (☎6594 3602; 2 Guanghua Dongli; 光华东里2号; mains ¥30-50; ⏱11am-10.30pm; ⑤Jintaixizhao) has been serving up its reasonably priced medley of dishes (the Peking duck is especially good value) from across China for almost 20 years at this three-storey venue. It's down an alley off Guanghua Lu.

④ **Shard Box Store** 慎德阁

Using porcelain fragments from Ming and Qing dynasty vases that were destroyed during the Cultural Revolution, this fascinating family-run **store** (4 Ritan Beilu 日坛北路4号; ⏱9am-7pm;

⑤Yong'anli) creates beautiful and unique shard boxes, bottles and jewellery. The boxes range from the tiny (¥30), for storing rings or cufflinks, to the large (¥8000). It also repairs and sells jewellery, mostly sourced from Tibet and Mongolia.

⑤ **The Place** 世贸天阶

Beijing has gone mall-mad in recent years; it seems that a new one opens every week. But we like **The Place** (9a Guanghua Lu 光华路甲9号; ⏱10am-10pm; ⑤Yong'anli) for the spectacular and giant video screen that looks down on you (an object of fascination for kids), as well as for the decent mix of mid-range brands such as Zara and French Connection that the locals love.

⑥ **China World Shopping Mall** 国贸商城

Packed with top-name brands, including Burberry, Marc Jacobs and Prada, as well as boutiques and jewellery stores, **China World** (1 Jianguomenwai Dajie 建国门外大街1号; ⏱10am-9.30pm; ⑤Guomao) is one of the more popular malls in Beijing. There's also an ice rink in the basement, so if you feel like a skating break you know where to go.

A **B** **C** **D**

Zhihua Temple
2
Lumicang
Hutong
Yabao Lu
Ritan Beilu
1
Jintaixizhao
金台西照
1 CCTV
Building
Chaoyang Dajie

Guanghua Lu 光华路

Dongdaqiao Lu

Ritan Lu
Ritan Park
Ritán Dongl

Guanghua Lu
光华路
6

JIÀNGUÓMÉNWÀI
EMBASSY AREA

Dongsanhuan
Zhonglu (East
3rd Ring Rd)
东三环北路

Jianguomen Beidajie

Xiushui Beijie

Xiushui Nanjie
5

Jianguomenwai Dajie
Jianguomen
建国门
7

建国门外大街

Yong'anli
永安里
3

Guomao
国贸

Jianguo Lu

Dawanglu
大望路

2

Tonghui River

Guangqumen Nanbinhe Lu

Baqiao Dajie

Dongsanhuan Zhonglu
(East 3rd Ring Rd)
东三环中路

3

Guangqumenwai Dajie 广渠门外大街

Guanghe L

Huacheng River (City Moat)

Guangqumen Nanbinhe Lu

Guanghe Lu

Xizhaosi Jie

Guanghe Dongjie

Chuiyangliu
Zhongjie

Chuiyangliu Nanjie

Shuangjing
双井

Guangqu Lu

4

Guangming Lu

Guanghe Dongjie

Jingsong Lu

Jinsong
劲松

Jinsong
劲松

Nanmofang Lu

Dongsanhuan Nanlu
东三环南路

Jinsong Nanlu

0   500 m
0   0.25 miles

Zuo anmennei Dajie

Longtan Lu 龙潭路

Longtan Park

Panjiayuan Donglu

Panjiayuan Lu

**Panjiayuan
Antique Market**

8

5

For reviews see	
Top Sights	p86
Sights	p91
Eating	p91
Drinking	p92
Shopping	p93

Sights

CCTV Building
ARCHITECTURE

1 Map p90, C2

The headquarters for China Central TV is like no other building in the city, or anywhere else. This Dutch-designed behemoth, known to the locals as 'big underpants', with its open centre, seemingly defies gravity. Gardens around the complex were being landscaped at the time of writing, so by the time you read this you should be able to wander beneath the monster. (央视大楼; 32 Dongsanhuan Zhonglu 东三环中路 32号; **S** Jintaixizhao)

Zhihua Temple
BUDDHIST TEMPLE

2 Map p90, A1

With its distinctive black-tiled roofs and an air of dilapidated grandeur, this little-visited Ming-era temple is an oasis of calm in the busy downtown area. The highlight is the Tathagata Hall, with its cabinets for storing sutras and statues of the Sakyamuni Buddha. (智化寺; 5 Lumicang Hutong 禄米仓胡同 5号; admission ¥20; 9am-4.30pm Tue-Sun; **S** Jianguomen or Chaoyangmen)

Eating

Najia Xiaoguan
CHINESE MANCHU $$

3 Map p90, B2

This is a fun courtyard restaurant that bubbles with old-Beijing atmos-

phere and bases its menu on an old imperial Manchu recipe book called the *Golden Soup Bible*. The imperial Manchu theme sounds a tad tacky, but it's carried off in a fun but tasteful way. At peak times, be prepared to wait for a table; it's worth it. (那家小馆; 6567 3663; 10 Yong'an Xili, off Jianguomenwai Dajie 建国门外大街永安西里 10号; mains ¥40-70; 11am-9.30pm; **S** Yong'anli;)

Din Tai Fung
CHINESE DUMPLINGS $$

4 Map p90, D2

Very special dumplings are the draw here; the original restaurant of this Taiwanese chain was once hailed as one of the 10 best in the world by the *New York Times*. Try the *xiaolongbao*,

---

Local Life
Ritan Park

One of Beijing's most pleasant parks, beautifully landscaped **Ritan** (日坛公园; Ritan Lu; admission free; 6am-9pm; **S** Chaoyangmen) makes a lovely city-centre escape and is superb for watching the locals at play. Activities include dancing, singing, kite flying, rock climbing (¥30 to ¥50), table tennis and pond fishing (¥5 per hour). Otherwise, just stroll around and enjoy the flora, or head to the southwest of the park to the **Stone Boat** (石舫咖啡; beers & coffee from ¥25, cocktails from ¥35; 10am-10pm), a popular cafe in the day and chilled bar at night.

thin-skinned packages with meat or veggie fillings that are surrounded by a superb, scalding soup. (鼎泰丰; ☎6553 1536; 6th fl, Shin Kong Pl, 87 Jianguo Lu 建国路87号新光天地 6层; dumplings ¥20-70; ⏰11.30am-9.30pm Mon-Fri, 11am-10pm Sat & Sun; S Dawanglu; 🚭 ⓔ)

Makye Ame

TIBETAN $$

5 Map p90, A1

With its nightly Tibetan dancing show, this is a loud and fun place that serves up lots of yak meat, *momo* (Tibetan dumplings) and *tsampa,* the roasted barley meal that is a Tibetan staple, in a welcoming atmosphere. Book ahead at weekends. (玛吉阿米; ☎6506 9616; 2nd fl, 11a Xiushui Nanjie 秀水南街甲 11号 2层; dishes from ¥30; ⏰11.30am-midnight; S Yong'anli)

Drinking

Haze

CLUB

6 Map p90, B1

In the corner of a tower block with a striking Swiss cheese–like facade, this funky basement club, with stylish bar at ground level above it, gets lively on weekends, with mostly house music. The steep, spiral staircase leading down to the club is lethal after a few drinks. (A101 Guanghua Lu Soho, Guanghua Lu 光华路光华路Soho地下1层; club admission ¥50; ⏰11pm-6am; S Yong'anli)

Lan, designed by Philippe Starck

Lan

BAR

7 �’ Map p90, B2

You'll find paintings that dangle from the ceiling, giant mirrors against the walls and fin-de-siècle–style furniture here, as well as the most extravagant toilets in the city. They all make this Philippe Starck–designed bar Beijing's most eye-catching nightlife destination. (兰会所; 4th fl, LG Twin Towers Shopping Mall B-12, Jianguomenwai Dajie 建国门外大街乙12号双子座大厦 4层; cocktails from ¥50; ⏱11am-2am; 🅂Yong'anli)

Shopping

Beijing Curio City

MARKET

8 🔒 Map p90, C5

Four floors of antiques, jewellery, ceramics, carpets and furniture are available here in a more low-key atmosphere than in many Beijing markets. Not all the antiques are the real deal, though, so look carefully before you buy and haggle as hard as you can. (北京古玩城; 21 Dongsanhuan Nanlu 东三环南路 21号; ⏱10am-6pm; 🅂Jinsong)

Local Life

High Life

If you want to enjoy a sweeping view over the city while eating a meal or downing a drink, then head to the gargantuan but not very romantically named **China World Trade Centre Phase Three** (1 Jianguomenwai Dajie 建国门外大街1号国贸大酒店; 🅂 Guomao), Beijing's tallest building. If the credit card isn't maxed out yet, eat at **Grill 79** (国贸79; 79th fl China World Trade Centre Phase Three; mains ¥180-300; ⏱noon-2pm & 6-10pm; 🅂Guomao; 🌱🍴), where the steaks are superb. Afterwards, head up one more floor to **Atmosphere** (云酷酒吧; 80th fl China World Summit Wing; cocktails from ¥80; ⏱noon-2am; 🅂Guomao) for cocktails, Cuban cigars and live jazz. The World Trade centre is just to the northwest of Guomao metro station.

Explore

The Summer Palace & Haidian

The glorious Summer Palace (颐和园) may be its principal sight, but there's far more to Haidian (海淀), which sprawls across west and northwest Beijing, than just old imperial digs. The district is home to the capital's biggest parks, while the hip student neighbourhood of Wudaokou (五道口) makes for a very lively contrast with the temples and museums you'll also find here.

The Sights in a Day

☀️ Your first stop has to be the **Summer Palace** (p96). Spend the morning exploring the former imperial playground and its tranquil and beautiful collection of gardens, temples and pavilions. Make sure to climb **Longevity Hill** (p97) for views across the capital, and promenade around the shores of **Kunming Lake** (p98).

☀️ Head to the **Fragrant Hills** (p123), where there are numerous places for lunch on the road to the north gate, and wander the trails, making sure to stop in at the **Azure Clouds Temple** (p123). Alternatively, temple-hop through some of Haidian's standout shrines, such as the **Wanshou Temple** (p102) and the **Wuta Temple** (p102).

🌙 In the evening, make tracks for **Wudaokou** (p102), the capital's student heartland. There are lots of buzzing cafes and bars here to start or end the night in, as well as some of Beijing's best Korean and Japanese eateries. You could also check out the **Golden Peacock** (p105), just one of the many ethnic minority restaurants serving up cuisines from across China that cluster in the Weigongcun area, north of the National Library metro station.

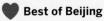

👁 Top Sights
Summer Palace (p96)

❤️ Best of Beijing

Best Food
Golden Peacock (p105)

Salang Bang (p104)

Best Drinking & Nightlife
Lush (p102)

Best Temples
Wanshou Temple (p102)

Wuta Temple (p102)

Azure Clouds Temple (p123)

Getting There

Ⓢ **Subway** Take Line 4 to Xiyuan for the Summer Palace. Use the National Library stop on the same line for the Wanshou and Wuta Temples. Line 4 also runs to Weigongcun and its ethnic minority restaurants. Take Line 13 for the Great Bell Temple and Wudaokou.

🚌 **Bus** The 331 links Wudaokou with the Summer Palace and Fragrant Hills Park.

Top Sights
Summer Palace

The splendid regal encampment of the Summer Palace (颐和园; Yihe Yuan) is one of Beijing's must-see sights. This former playground for the imperial court fleeing the insufferable summer torpor of the old imperial city is a marvel of landscaping: a wonderful, over-the-top mix of temples, gardens, pavilions, lakes, bridges, gate-towers and corridors. Packed with stunning individual sights, it's a fine place just to amble around in the sunshine, while the views from here are some of the best in all Beijing.

👁 off Map p100

Yiheyuan Lu 颐和园路

park only/park & palace ¥30/60, audio guide ¥40 (with ¥100 deposit)

🕗 8.30am-5pm

Ⓢ Xiyuan

Buddhist Fragrance Pavilion

Don't Miss

Hall of Benevolence & Longevity 仁寿殿
The main building at ground level, this **hall** (*Renshou Dian*) sits by the east gate and houses a hardwood throne. Look for the bronze animals that decorate the courtyard in front, including the mythical *qilin* (a hybrid animal that appeared on earth only at times of harmony).

The Long Corridor 长廊
Awesome in its conception and execution, the **Long Corridor** (*Chang Lang*) is absolutely unmissable. It stretches for over 700m and its beams, walls and some of the ceiling are decorated with 14,000 intricate paintings depicting scenes from Chinese history and myths, as well as Chinese literature's classic texts. Your neck will ache from all that staring upwards, but the pain is worth it.

Longevity Hill 万寿山
The slopes of this 60m-high hill are covered in temples and pavilions, all arranged on a north–south axis. The most prominent and important are the **Buddhist Fragrance Pavilion** and the **Cloud-Dispelling Hall**, which are connected by corridors. Awaiting you at the peak of the hill is the **Buddhist Temple of the Sea of Wisdom**. On a clear day, there are splendid views of Beijing from here.

Marble Boat 石舫
The **Marble Boat** (*Shifang*) has come to symbolise the extravagance and otherworldliness of the emperors in the final days of imperial rule. First built in 1755, it was restored in 1893 on the orders of Empress Cixi using money meant to go towards building real ships for the Chinese navy!

☑ Top Tips

▶ Boats ply Kunming Lake (p98), but you can hire a pedalo for ¥60 per hour (¥300 deposit) and float around at your own pace.

▶ The restaurants around the palace itself are expensive and mediocre.

▶ If you want to see all the sights inside, purchase the 'through ticket' (park and palace sights). Otherwise, the park ticket only allows you to wander the grounds and lake.

▶ As with all major sights in Beijing, try not to come here at weekends or on public holidays when the crowds can be oppressive.

✗ Take a Break

Nearby Wudaokou (p102) is your best option for a lunch break. Try **Salang Bang** (p104) for tasty Korean food, or the sushi bar at **Isshin** (p104).

Much of it is actually wood painted to look like marble.

Kunming Lake 昆明湖

Three-quarters of the palace complex is made up of the shallow Kunming Lake *(Kunming Hu)*, which was modelled on the famed West Lake in Hangzhou. Apart from the **Marble Boat** moored on the northwestern shore, note the nearby Qing dynasty boathouses and the **Gate Tower of the Cloud-Retaining Eves**, which once housed an ancient silver statue of Guanyu – the god of war.

West Causeway 西堤

A great way to escape the crowds that converge here is to strike out along the **West Causeway** (Xidi) and then do a circuit of the lake by returning along the east shore. The causeway is lined with delightful willow and mulberry trees, and along the way you'll come across the grey-and-white marble **Jade Belt Bridge**, which dates from the 18th century.

South Lake Island 南湖岛

Linked to the lakeshore by the graceful **17-Arch Bridge**, this island houses a fine **Dragon King Temple**, where the emperors used to come and pray for rain in times of drought. At sunset, the nearby east shore is popular with photographers looking for a spectacular shot of the sun disappearing behind the hills. You can also get here by boat (¥15).

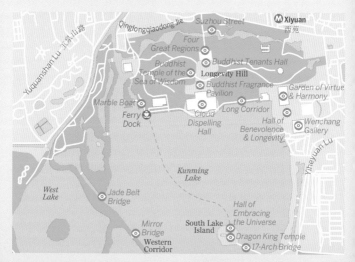

Understand
The Rise & Fall & Rise of the Summer Palace

It was the Qing emperor Qianlong who created the Summer Palace on the site of what had long been a royal garden, which was then known by the romantic, but not very regal, name of the 'Garden of Clear Ripples'. With the same determination he displayed expanding China's borders, Qianlong enlisted 100,000 workers in 1749 to enlarge the gardens and deepen Kunming Lake, while giving Longevity Hill its name in honour of his mother's 60th birthday.

Thankfully, Qianlong was long dead by the time British and French soldiers rampaged through the palace in 1860 at the end of the Second Opium War. Apart from pillaging anything not nailed down, they trashed many of the temples and pavilions. That left Empress Cixi to restore it to its former glory, and to re-name the complex the 'Summer Palace', only for foreign soldiers to return again in 1900 in the wake of the Boxer Rebellion, when yet more damage was done. Not until after 1949 and the communist takeover did work begin to repair this damage.

Wenchang Gallery 文昌阁
South of the main entrance; come here to take at look at Empress Cixi's handwriting (some of her calligraphy is on display), as well as porcelain, bronzes and a jade gallery. Various other Qing-era artefacts are on show as well.

E

WŬDÀOKŎU

9 ❌

Huanqing Lu

Shuangqing Lu

8 ❌
7 ❌ Wudaokou
五道口

Zhongguancun Donglu

日本料理一心

Zhichunlu
知春路

Zhichunli
知春里

D

Chengfu Lu

Beisihuan Xilu (North Fourth Ring Rd)

Zhichun Lu

Old Summer
Palace

6 ◉

C

Zhongguancun
Beidajie

East Gate of
Peking University
北京大学东门

Zhongguancun
中关村 🏠 10

Haidian
Huangzhuang
海淀黄庄

B

Yuanmingyuan
Park
圆明园

Qinghua Xilu
清华西路

Arthur M.Sackler
Museum of Art &
Archaeology

4 ◉

Peking
University

Haidian Lu

Suzhou L

Suzhouie
苏州街

A

Summer
Palace

Xiyuan
西苑

Yiheyuan Lu 颐和园路

Yiheyuan Lu
颐和园路

Yiheyuan Lu

Wanquanhe Lu

1

2

3

4

Great Bell
Temple **⑤**

Beisanhuan Xilu
北三环西路

Zhongguancun Donglu　日本料理一心

Xueyuan Nanlu
学院南路

Daliushu Lu
大柳树路

North
Jiaotong
University

Gaoliangqiao Xiejie
高梁桥斜街

HǎiDIÀN

Wuta Temple **②**

Běijīng
Zoo

Zhongguancun Nandajie
人民大学

exueyuan Nanlu

Weigongcun
魏公村 Ⓢ

Zhungguancun Nandajie

National Library
(Guojia Tushuguan) Ⓢ
国家图书馆

Zizhuyuán Park

Zhongguancun Nandajie

Weigong Jie

Weigongcun Lu

Wanshou
si Temple **①**

Wanshousi Lu 万寿寺路

Xisanhuan Beilu 西三环北路

③

Zizhuyuan Lu 紫竹院路

For reviews see	
⊙ Top Sights	p96
⊙ Sights	p102
✕ Eating	p104
🛍 Shopping	p105

1 km
0.5 miles

Sights

Wanshou Temple

BUDDHIST TEMPLE

1 Map p100, C8

This Ming dynasty–era temple has a fascinating history; this was where the emperors used to stop en route to the Summer Palace for a tea break. It was originally consecrated for the storage of Buddhist texts, but the temple now houses a fine collection of bronze Buddhist statues, as well as some magnificent stone and clay sculptures. (万寿寺; Suzhou Jie; admission ¥20; ⏰9am-4pm Tue-Sun; Ⓢ National Library)

Ⓠ Local Life

Wudaokou

With many of Beijing's universities in the area, Wudaokou (五道口) is the capital's student central. The main drag of Chengfu Lu buzzes at all hours and is home to bars, cafes and restaurants, as well as an outdoor beer garden set up by the subway stop in the summer. Try **Lush** (☏8286 3566; 2nd fl, 1 Huaqing Jiayuan, Chengfu Lu 成府路花清嘉园1楼2层; beers/cocktails from ¥15/35; ⏰24hr; Ⓢ Wudaokou; 🖫🖥), which hosts different events each night, or the nearby **Bridge Café** (桥咖啡; ☏8286 7025; 12-8 Huaqing Jiayuan 华清嘉园12-8; dishes from ¥32; ⏰24hr; Ⓢ Wudaokou; 🖫🖥).

Wuta Temple

BUDDHIST TEMPLE

2 Map p100, D8

With its unique five-pagoda roof, this secluded Ming-era structure looks more like an Indian temple than a Chinese one. The complex also holds a rare collection of stone statues, some scattered around the grounds, others stored carefully in the buildings to the back. (五塔寺; 24 Wutasi Cun 五塔寺村24号; admission ¥20, audio guide ¥10; ⏰9am-4pm; Ⓢ National Library)

Military Museum

MUSEUM

3 Map p100, off B8

This museum was undergoing a massive refit at the time of writing, but its forecourt bristled with a display of tanks, planes and artillery pieces that was free to see. When the building itself re-opens, you'll find everything from swords to surface-to-air missiles inside. Despite the martial tone, this is one of Beijing's more popular museums. (军事博物馆; 9 Fuxing Lu; admission ¥20; ⏰8am-5pm Tue-Sun, last entry 4.30pm; Ⓢ Military Museum (Junshibowuguan)

Arthur M Sackler Museum of Art & Archaeology

MUSEUM

4 Map p100, C1

Excellent collection of relics housed on the campus of Peking University. Exhibits include the Jinniushan Man (a 280,000-year-old skeleton), bronze artefacts, jade pieces and a host of other relics from primordial China. Afterwards make sure to wander

Great Bell Temple

around the pleasant campus, a refreshing break from Beijing's frantic mayhem. (赛克勒考古与艺术博物馆; Peking University west entrance 北京大学西门; admission free; ⊙9am-4.30pm; ⑤East Gate of Peking University)

Great Bell Temple

BUDDHIST TEMPLE

5 ◎ Map p100, E5

Ring the bell here and half of Beijing will hear it; the centrepiece of this temple, which was once where emperors came to pray for rain, is a massive Ming-dynasty bell that weighs in at almost 50 tonnes. There's also a huge array of less imposing bells, all inscribed with delicate characters.

There's an audio-guide available for ¥10, although earplugs might be more suitable. (大钟寺; 31a Beisanhuan Xilu 北三环西路甲31号; admission ¥20; ⊙9am-4.30pm Tue-Sun; ⑤Dazhongsi)

Old Summer Palace

PARK/RUINS

6 ◎ Map p100, C1

Not to be confused with the Summer Palace (p96), this once glorious complex of European-style buildings was sacked by Anglo-French forces in 1860 during the Second Opium War, a humiliation the Chinese have still not forgotten. Now, you can wander through the melancholy ruins and then stroll on through the massive park that surrounds them. (圆明园; 28 Qinghua Xilu; park only/all sights ¥10/25, map ¥6; ⏰7am-7pm; Ⓢ Yuanmingyuan Park)

Eating

Salang Bang

KOREAN $

7 🍴 Map p100, E2

It's one of the most popular and lively of the many Korean eateries in this area, and always busy with expat Korean students looking for a taste of home. The various hotpots, including the classic *shiguo banfan* (rice, vegetables, meat and an egg served in a claypot), start at ¥35, or grill your own meat and fish at your table. Pic-

ture menu. (舍廊房; ☎8261 8201; 3rd fl, Dongyuan Plaza, 35 Chengfu Lu; 成府路35号东源大厦3层; dishes from ¥25; ⏰10.30am-3.30am; Ⓢ Wudaokou)

Isshin

JAPANESE $

8 🍴 Map p100, E2

A favourite with locals and expats, Isshin serves affordable sushi and sashimi, as well as top-notch hotpots and teriyaki dishes, in cool, dark surroundings. The set lunch is a decent deal. The entrance is just off Shuang-qing Lu (双清路) north of Chengfu Lu. Turn left through the big arch. (日本料理一心; ☎6257 4853; West Bldg, 35 Chengfu Lu 成府路35号院内西楼; sushi from ¥12; ⏰lunch & dinner; Ⓢ Wudaokou; 📖)

CHRISTIAN KOBER/GETTY IMAGES ©

Military Museum (p102)

Lao Che Ji

CHINESE SICHUAN $$

9 Map p100, E2

The speciality here is *malaxiangguo* (麻辣香锅), a kind of dry hotpot where you add your own meat, fish and veggies, but it comes without the bubbling broth you get with standard hotpot. You can choose from three different levels of spice; go for the lowest if you can't handle the heat. Has a picture menu. (老车记; ☑ 6266 6180; 5th fl, Wudaokou U-Centre, 36 Chengfu Lu 成府路 36号五道口购物中心5层; meals for 2 ¥70; ⏰ 10am-10pm; ⑤ Wudaokou)

Shopping

Centergate Como

COMPUTERS & ELECTRONICS

10 🔒 Map p100, C3

Zhongguancun is China's Silicon Valley and this vast mall is the place to come for Beijing's cheapest range of computer software and hardware, games, cell phones, mp3 players; just about any IT product you could want. Not all of it is the genuine article, but you can bargain here. Go to the 2nd floor for laptop repairs. (科贸电子城; 18 Zhongguancun Dajie 中关村大街18号; ⏰ 9am-7pm; ⑤ Zhongguancun)

◯ Local Life

Ethnic Eats in Weigongcun

China has a special university (民族大学; *Minzu Daxue*) for its many ethnic minorities, and on nearby Weigong Jie you'll find some of the most authentic restaurants serving up their local cuisines. There's everything from Mongolian to Tibetan and Uighur food here. But perhaps the best option is the wonderful **Golden Peacock** (金孔雀德宏傣味餐厅; ☑ 6893 2030; Weigongcun 魏公村韦伯豪家园南门对 面; dishes from ¥18; ⏰ 11am-10pm; ⑤ Weigongcun; 🅿), which specialises in the Southeast Asian–like cuisine of the Dai people from the southwestern province of Yunnan. To get here, jump on Line 4 to Weigongcun and then walk south down Zhungguanancun for 400m to Weigongcun.

Top Sights
The Great Wall

Getting There

🚌 **Bus** 877, 919 and 880 (¥12; 6am to 6.30pm) leave for Badaling from Deshengmen Gate Tower.

🚆 **Train** Four morning trains (75min) leave from Beijing North Station (北京北站).

The most iconic monument in all China, the Great Wall (长城; *Changcheng*) stands as an awe-inspiring symbol of the grandeur of China's past. There's no way you can leave Beijing without having set foot on its ancient ramparts. Badaling (八达岭) is the closest stretch of the wall to the capital and, despite the inevitable crowds, it is highly photogenic, with fine watchtowers and, best of all, the classic vista of the wall snaking off across the hills into the far distance.

A section of the Great Wall at Badaling

Don't Miss

Hiking the Wall

The Badaling section of the Wall dates back to the Ming dynasty (1368–1644), but was heavily restored between the 1950s and '80s. This makes it one of the better places to hike the Wall, because what's underfoot isn't crumbling away; from the main entrance, you can walk east or west for some distance before you hit the unrestored sections. Bear in mind the Wall is steep, so wear sensible shoes and take water with you.

Watchtowers

The soldiers guarding what was then China's frontier lived and worked in the impressive watchtowers (*dilou*) interspersed along the Wall here. They weren't just defensive fortifications; a system of smoke signals, generated by burning wolves' dung, was used to transmit information along the wall and back to Beijing itself.

China Great Wall Museum 中国长城博物馆

Included in the ticket price is entrance to this **museum** (⏱9am-4pm Tue-Sun), which offers a comprehensive history of the Wall from its origins as an earthen embankment in the far-off Qin dynasty (221–206 BC), to the Ming-era battlements you see today. It's a good way to get a sense of just how astonishing and extensive a structure the Wall is.

Winter Wall

If you're in Beijing in the winter, then that's by far the best time to visit Badaling. You'll have the place almost to yourself, and the snow that covers the ramparts makes the Wall even more picturesque. The downside is that you will need to wrap up like an Inuit. Due to elevation and

---

70km from Beijing

adult/student ¥45/25

⏱summer 6am-7pm, winter 7am-6pm

☑ Top Tips

▸ Every hostel and many hotels in Beijing offer day trips to Badaling; they're often the most convenient way to visit.

▸ Give the despicable Bear Park a very wide berth.

▸ There's a Bank of China ATM near the west car park.

▸ Combine a trip here with a visit to the Ming Tombs (p109).

✖ Take a Break

There are dozens of restaurants here. Try **Yonghe King** (永和大王; mains ¥10-20; ⏱10am-9pm; 🅟) for Chinese fast food: rice meals, dumplings, noodles.

Understand

Great Wall of China

Dating back 2000-odd years, the Great Wall stretches for an estimated 8851km as it snakes from the border with North Korea in the east, to Lop Nur in the far western province of Xinjiang. Meandering its way through 17 provinces, principalities and autonomous regions, the Wall started out as a line of defence against the Mongol hordes. It has had no practical use for centuries, but its grip on the imagination of both locals and foreigners remains as strong as ever.

History

The Wall wasn't built in one go. Rather, there are four distinct Walls. Work on the 'original' began during the Qin dynasty (221–207 BC), when hundreds of thousands of workers laboured for 10 years to construct it. An estimated 180 million cubic metres of rammed earth was used to form the core of this Wall, along with, legend has it, the bones of dead workers.

Work continued during the Han dynasty (206 BC–AD 220) but it took the impending threat of Genghis Khan to spur further construction in the Jin dynasty (1115–1234). The Wall's final incarnation, the one most people see today, came during the Ming dynasty (1368–1644), when it was reinforced with stone, brick and battlements over a period of 100 years.

Despite being home to around one million soldiers, the great irony of the Wall is that it rarely stopped China's enemies from invading. It was never one continuous structure; there were inevitable gaps and it was through those that Genghis Khan rode in to take Beijing in 1215. Nor could the Wall stop the Manchus sweeping down from what is now northeastern China and overthrowing the Ming dynasty in 1644.

Ruin & Restoration

With the Mongol threat long gone, the Wall became increasingly redundant during the Qing dynasty and fell into disrepair. Its degeneration continued after the communist takeover of 1949. In 1984 it was placed under government protection. Despite much restoration work, huge sections of the Wall are nothing more than rubble, or mounds of earth. Only around Beijing do lucky visitors see the Wall in something approaching its former glory.

exposure, Badaling is far colder than Beijing and the wind up here cuts like a knife.

The Countryside
One of the joys of a trip to the Wall is that it gets you out of the city and into the fresh air of the countryside. The landscape around Badaling is especially raw and striking, a real contrast to where you've come from. Note how many of the village houses around Badaling are made out of bricks pillaged from the Wall!

The Ming Tombs 十三陵
Often included in a tour to Badaling is a visit to the **Ming Tombs** (Changchi Lu, Changping 明昌平区昌赤路; full admission ¥180, per sight ¥35-65; ⊙8am-5.30pm; 🚍872), 20km away. Beijing's answer to Egypt's Valley of the Kings is the final resting place for 13 of the 16 Ming emperors; the approach to the tombs is via the remarkable 7km-long **Spirit Way**, lined with stone statues of animals and court officials.

Simatai 司马台
If the Wall at Badaling only whets the appetite, the stirring remains at **Simatai** (admission ¥40; ⊙8am-5pm; 🚍980, then minibus or taxi), 110km northeast of Beijing, make for an exhilarating

Pavilion at the Ming Tombs

Great Wall experience. Built during the reign of Ming dynasty emperor Hongwu, the 19km stretch of wall here is characterised by watchtowers, sharp plunges and scrambling ascents. It's a partly restored, yet very rugged, strip of Wall and it can be heart-thumpingly steep in places. Needless to say, the scenery is dramatic.

The Best of
Beijing

Acrobats performing at Chaoyang Theatre (p81)
GREG ELMS/GETTY IMAGES ©

Best Walks
Tiananmen Square & Foreign Legation Quarter

🏃 The Walk

Tucked away to the southeast of Tiananmen Square is the fascinating former Foreign Legation Quarter. The peaceful, tree-lined streets here are lined with European-style buildings from the late 19th and early 20th centuries, which were once the homes and offices of the small Western community in old Peking. The quarter is a real oasis in this part of town and great for a wander.

Start Tiananmen Square

Finish Raffles Beijing Hotel

Length 1 hour; 2km

🍴 Take a Break

For solid Sichuan dishes served up in old-world surroundings, you can't go past the former French post office that dates back to 1901, **Jingyuan Chuancai** (静园川菜; 19 Dongjiaomin Xiang 东交民巷 19号; mains ¥20-50; ⏱10.30am-2pm & 4.30-9.30pm; Ⓢ Qianmen, Tiananmen East or Wangfujing; 📖).

Beijing Police Museum (p41)

TAO IMAGES LIMITED/GETTY IMAGES ©

❶ Tiananmen Square

Start your walk at the symbolic centre of the Chinese universe, **Tiananmen Square** (p30).

❷ French Hospital

Leaving the square, cross the road and climb the 16 steps into Dongjiaomin Xiang, once known as Legation St. The red-brick building next to the Tian'an Hotel at No 39 was the former French Hospital.

❸ Legation Quarter

A little further on, through a grey-brick archway on your right, stands the elegant former Legation Quarter. Formerly the US embassy until 1949, and then briefly the Beijing residence of the Dalai Lama, it has now been converted into a trendy restaurant zone.

❹ Beijing Police Museum

Further along on your right is a building with massive neo-classical pillars, the erstwhile address of the First

National City Bank of New York. It's now the quirky and fun **Beijing Police Museum** (p41).

❺ French Legation

Keep walking east and you'll pass a domed building on the corner of Zhengyi Lu and Dongjiaomin Xiang, once the Yokohama Specie Bank. You can grab lunch at Jingyuan Chuancai, the old French post office, and then head on to the former French Legation. The main gate, at No 15, is a large red entrance guarded by a pair of stone lions and impassive security guards.

❻ St Michael's

The twin spires of the Gothic St Michael's Church rise ahead at No 11, facing the green roofs and ornate red brickwork of the old Belgian Legation. It's still a working church and always busy at Easter and Christmas.

❼ Rue Hart

Stroll north along Taijichang Dajie and hunt down the brick street sign embedded in the northern wall of Taijichang Toutiao, carved with the old name of the road, Rue Hart. On the north side of Rue Hart was the Austro-Hungarian Legation, south of which stood the Peking Club.

❽ Raffles Beijing

At the north end of Taijichang Dajie, across busy Dongchang'an Jie is the Raffles Beijing Hotel, housed in a building that dates to 1900.

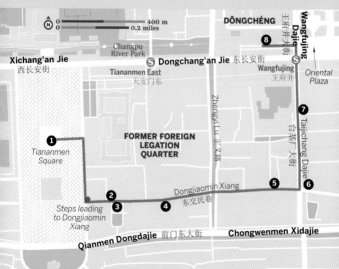

Best Walks
Forbidden City & Dongcheng Hutong

🏃 The Walk

This walk (which also makes a great bike ride) takes you through some of Beijing's oldest and most historic *hutong* and reveals as much about the capital as any museum. This was the heart of imperial Beijing, as well as the former stamping ground of the young Mao Zedong, so there's plenty to see.

Start Hong Lou

Finish Meridian Gate

Length 2½ hours (1½ hours if riding); 5km

🍴 Take a Break

Stock up on dumplings, either boiled or steamed, at Hangzhou Xiaochi (p25). There are also good soups and noodles here.

BEST VIEW STOCK/GETTY IMAGES ©

Forbidden City (p24)

❶ Hong Lou

Head for the imperial *hutong* east of **Jingshan Park** (p41), passing en route the 1918 red-brick building **Hong Lou**. It was once the library and arts department of Peking University; Mao Zedong used to work here as a librarian in the days before he was running China.

❷ Mao Zedong's Former Home

Turn right into Shatan Beijie then left into Songzhuyuan Xixiang. Bear right, then turn left into Sanyanjing Hutong. Just before the end, turn right into Jiansuo Zuoxiang to find Mao Zedong's former home at No 8. He lived here while working at the university library.

❸ Former Home of Imperial Eunuch Li Lianyin

At the end of the alley, turn left, then second right and head left towards Huanghuamen Jie. No 43 is the former courtyard home of the imperial eunuch Li Lianyin, a favourite of Empress Dowager Cixi.

At the end, turn right then left under an arch into Youqizuo Hutong.

❹ Eastern Wall of Beihai Park

Now the *hutong* twists and turns get fun. Turn right, then left at the end, then right at the end beside No 46, then bear left, then right, turn left at the end and finally turn left onto Gongjian Hutong – still with us? Soon after, turn right into Gongjian 2 Hutong, which hugs the huge grey-bricked eastern wall of Beihai Park (p58).

❺ Forbidden City Moat

You'll eventually pop out onto Jingshan Xijie. Follow this road to the west gate of Jingshan Park, but turn right and then go under the arch in the far end of the car park, which takes you into Dashizuo Hutong, a wiggly alley which wends its way to Jingshan Qianjie. Once there, you'll see the Forbidden City moat right in front of you.

❻ Meridian Gate

Follow Beichang Jie past the now-closed **Fuyou Temple** and opposite, at No 39, the entranceway to the disused **Wanshou Xinglong Temple**, which dates from the 1700s. Then turn left at the west gate of Forbidden City and follow the moat to the Meridian Gate.

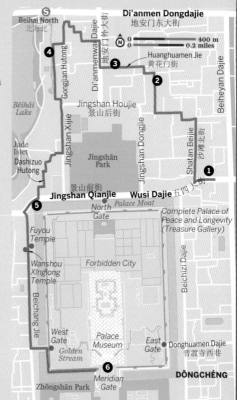

Best Cycles
Houhai Lakes Bike Ride

🏃 The Cycle

This very gentle bike ride, all on the flat, whips you round the Houhai lakes and some of the surrounding *hutong*. There are little-visited temples to discover, as well as two of Beijing's most impressive and historic residential compounds to explore. You could easily walk this route as well.

Start Yandai Xiejie

Finish Di'anmen Xidajie

Length 2 hours (3 hours if walking); 5km

🍴 Take a Break

Yangfang Hutong is full of little restaurants that make good lunch spots. Otherwise, try Kong Yiji (p67), although if you're on your bike, go easy on the dishes doused in their trademark sherry-like wine.

Prince Gong's Residence (p47)

LONELY PLANET/GETTY IMAGES ©

❶ Yandai Xiejie

Start at the Di'anmenwai Dajie end of Yandai Xiejie, pedalling slowly past name chop vendors, Tibetan silver trinket sellers, bars and cafes. Go straight on at the end of the street and you enter Ya'er Hutong.

❷ Guanghua Temple

Ride on and you'll find the Buddhist Guanghua Temple, which dates from the far-off Yuan dynasty. At the end of the *hutong,* turn left into a narrow alley which will take you to Houhai Beiyan. Turn right again and almost immediately you'll pass the former **Dazanglonghua Temple**, built in 1719 and now a kindergarten.

❸ Song Qingling Former Residence

Push on along Houhai Beiyan and you'll come to the Song Qingling Former Residence. Song is venerated by the Chinese as the wife of Sun Yat-sen, founder of the Republic of China in 1912, and her house was once the home of the father of Puyi, China's last emperor. There's a lovely garden here and an interesting museum about Madame Song's life.

④ Xihai Lake

Turn left onto Houhai Xiyan and after 200m right onto an alley that connects with Deshengmennei Dajie. Go across that street and down the alley opposite, which leads you to Xihai Lake, the smallest of the three Houhai lakes but the most popular with local anglers.

⑤ Prince Gong's Residence

Circle the lake anti-clockwise and return to Deshengmennei Dajie. Turn right and head down it for 200m and then turn left into **Yangfang Hutong**, a good place to stop for coffee or lunch. Follow the *hutong* to the right and enter Liuyin Jie, which leads down to Prince Gong's Residence, perhaps the most impressive courtyard house in all Beijing.

⑥ Silver Ingot Bridge

Bear left at the end of Liuyin Jie and go onto Qianhai Xijie, which will take you to Qianhai Beiyan, the west shore of Qianhai Lake. Hug the lakeshore until you reach the Silver Ingot Bridge.

⑦ Di'anmen Xidajie

Cross Silver Ingot Bridge and turn sharp right. Carry along the east shore of Qianhai, passing **Yinding Bridge** on your left, until you reach Di'anmen Xidajie.

Best
Temples

There are temples scattered throughout every district in Beijing and each one is unique in its own way. It's well worth taking your time to visit several. By stepping through their gates, you leave the hustle of modern Beijing behind and enter a timeless world of solemn worshippers, busy monks and plumes of incense wafting through the air.

Layout

Every school of Chinese thought – Buddhist, Confucian, Taoist – is represented in Beijing's temples. The temples are laid out in the same way as traditional courtyard homes (p46), along a north–south axis according to the principles of feng shui. The middle courtyard area contains the prayer halls, while the surrounding quarters usually house the resident monks.

Buddhist, Taoist or Confucian?

The differences between Buddhist and Taoist temples aren't always immediately apparent, but the monks have distinctive appearances. Buddhist monks usually have shaved heads, while Taoists have their long hair tied into a topknot. Confucian temples will always have a prominent statue of Confucius himself.

Which Temple to Visit?

The colossal Temple of Heaven (p50) is the best-known shrine in the capital and sees the most visitors, but the Buddhist Lama Temple (p34) and Taoist White Cloud Temple (p64) attract the most worshippers. Smaller temples are invariably the most peaceful to visit, though the Confucius Temple (p40) is superbly serene despite being China's second-largest shrine to the famous philosopher.

TRAVELASIA/GETTY IMAGES ©

☑ Top Tips

▶ Beijing's temples welcome visitors, but always ask permission to take photos of the monks or worshippers.

Best Historic Temples

Temple of Heaven (p50) Awesome example of architectural perfection, with every part of the complex loaded with symbolic significance.

Fayuan Temple (p64) Lovely, ancient shrine that dates back to the 7th century and houses fine, restored statues.

Miaoying Temple White Dagoba (p64) This temple has loomed over the surrounding *hutong* since the Yuan dynasty (1206–1368).

Confucius Temple (p40)

White Cloud Temple (p64) Fantastic Taoist temple with over 1200 years of history behind it.

Azure Clouds Temple (p123) With its superbly evocative name, this is another welcome survivor from the Yuan dynasty.

Confucius Temple (p40) China's premier place of learning in the imperial era, infused with a suitably reverent atmosphere.

Zhihua Temple (p91) Little-visited, slightly ramshackle but very charming temple which offers the chance for serious contemplation.

Best Tibetan Temples

Lama Temple (p34) Hands down the most popular temple in town for local worshippers.

Wuta Temple (p102) A striking, secluded temple with a unique look that reveals the influence of India.

Best Unusual Temples

Dongyue Temple (p77) Disconcerting but fascinating shrine where tormented spirits writhe in the Taoist version of hell.

Wanshou Temple (p102) This place has been everything from a Buddhist storage house to a barracks and favourite stop of the emperors in its time.

Best
Parks & Gardens

Beijing's parks and gardens provide much-needed sanctuary in this increasingly steel- and glass-heavy city. With backyards a real rarity in apartment-centric Beijing, you'll find the locals in them from dawn to well after dusk. They're ideal for catching your breath in the middle of a hard day's shopping, or for shaking off the dust from palaces and temples.

LIU XIAOYANG/ALAMY ©

Royal Heritage

Many of Beijing's parks, like Beihai Park (p56) and Jingshan Park (p41), are former imperial gardens, or were used by the emperors to perform annual rituals. As such, they were off-limits to ordinary Beijingers. These days, however, many locals use them for kite flying and taichi.

But Chinese parks and gardens are more than just recreational spaces. They are regarded as landscape art and must have several elements – the main ones being plants, rocks, water and pavilions – to be considered harmonious.

Best Historic Parks

Temple of Heaven (p50)
A wonderful shady space lined with ancient and gnarled cypress trees.

Ritan Park (p91) The former temple of the sun and a superb example of landscaping.

Jingshan Park (p41)
The only place in central Beijing where you'll find a hill!

Best for Walking

Fragrant Hills Park
(p123) The best hiking in town can be found out here on Beijing's far northwestern fringe.

Old Summer Palace
(p103) Pass through the ruins of this palace and a massive park awaits.

Best for Fun

Beihai Park (p58) Join the communal dancing, practise taichi, or just have fun in a boat.

Houhai (p64) A playground during the day and a nightlife hub once the sun goes down.

Best
Museums &
Galleries

In keeping with Beijing's emergence as a true world city, the capital's museums and galleries have made great strides in the last few years. Now, Beijing can boast of being one of the most happening places on the planet for contemporary art, while scattered around town there are museums devoted to everything from ancient architecture to sandalwood.

Beijing's Museum Makeover

Once characterised by 'Chinglish' captions (or none at all), sullen staff and a deadening, lifeless atmosphere seemingly designed to send visitors to sleep, Beijing museums have been given a radical makeover since the 2008 Olympics. There are now a few, like the outstanding Capital Museum, which can rank with the best in Europe, while others, such as the Poly Art Museum, are amazing to visit just because of the incredible exhibits they house.

Best Exhibits

Capital Museum (p64)
The finest museum in town and a great guide to Beijing.

Poly Art Museum (p40)
Stunning bronzes and sublime statues dating back thousands of years.

National Museum of China (p31) Finally reopened to reveal its superb collection of antiquities.

Clock Exhibition Hall
(p26) Magnificent time-pieces amassed by the Qing emperors.

Best Galleries

Red Gate Gallery (p53)
The first gallery in Beijing devoted to contemporary art, and still one of the best.

UCCA (p72) Four massive spaces to explore at this influential and innovative arts centre.

TAO/ROBERT HARDING ©

☑ **Top Tips**

▶ Remember that many museums and most of the galleries in the 798 Art District (p72) are closed on Mondays, so plan ahead.

Quirkiest Collections

Beijing Police Museum
(p41) Explore the mean streets of old and new Beijing through the eyes of the local fuzz.

Military Museum (p102)
Swords and surface-to-air missiles, tanks, planes and good history, too.

Best
Imperial Beijing

Look around certain parts of Beijing, such as the mall- and skyscraper-dominated CBD and Sanlitun, and it's easy to forget the capital's imperial roots. But for all the changes wrought in the last 60-odd years, modern-day Beijing is still very much tied to old Peking: the city of emperors, mandarins and concubines, and their courtyard houses, *hutong* and palaces.

TAO IMAGES LIMITED/GETTY IMAGES ©

Beginnings

The Ming emperor Yongle turned Beijing into an imperial city, raising it from the rubble of the former Mongol capital in the early 15th century. Under Yongle's watch, the Forbidden City was built, along with the city walls, while the *hutong* were renovated. By the time the Ming dynasty fell in 1644, Beijing was home to over 2000 temples and was one of the most important and influential cities in all Asia. The Manchu warriors who established the subsequent Qing dynasty carried on the development, building the inner walls that divided their imperial, or 'Tartar', city from the so-called Chinese city beyond it.

Hutong Evolution

Hutong (p46) started to appear in Beijing in the Yuan dynasty (1271–1368), when the city was being run by the Mongols; the word '*hutong*' is believed to come from an old Mongol term for a passageway. They proliferated through the Ming and Qing dynasties, until there were estimated to be 6000 of them in the capital. Those numbers have dropped dramatically in recent years, as huge swathes of *hutong* land has been demolished to make way for apartment blocks, offices and roads. There are reckoned to be somewhere between 1000 and 2000 left.

Best Palaces & Royal Residences

Forbidden City (p24)
You can't really miss this one, can you?

Summer Palace (p96)
The Qing emperors' version of a holiday home, on a huge scale.

Lama Temple (p34)
Originally the home of a prince who got promoted to emperor.

Prince Gong's Residence (p116) This compound was so nice that the youngest son of Emperor Qianlong pinched it (after executing the owner).

Song Qingling Former Residence (p116) The father of Puyi, China's last emperor, lived here first.

Old Summer Palace (p103) The saddest imperial sight; wander the

Old Summer Palace (p103)

ruins and muse on how amazing this place must have looked.

Best Historic Hutong

Nanluogu Xiang (p42) Buzzing now with bars, cafes and restaurants, but 800 years of history behind it.

Guozijian Jie (p40) Home of the Confucius Temple and now a great spot for a coffee.

Mao'er Hutong (p42) Long favoured by senior officials; Wan Rong, the last empress of China, grew up here.

Zhonglouwan Hutong (p40) Many imperial eunuchs retired around here.

Dashilar (p60) Ancient shopping street.

Dazhalan Xijie (p61) The centre of old Peking's red-light district.

Shanxi Xiang (p61) The fantastic courtyard house here was once Beijing's smartest brothel.

Jiansuo Zuoxiang (p114) Mao Zedong lived here before he became China's chairman.

Best Imperial Temples

Temple of Heaven (p50) Emperors came here twice a year to pray for their subjects.

Confucius Temple (p40) Where mandarins studied the classics.

Wanshou Temple (p102) Favourite spot for an imperial tea break.

Worth a Trip

Once the royal hunting grounds, **Fragrant Hills Park** (香山公园; summer/winter ¥10/5; ◷6am-7.30pm; **S** Xiyuan or Yuanmingyuan Park, then 🚌331) is one of the great escapes for Beijingers. It's superb in the autumn, when the abundant maple leaves turn a flaming red. Near the north gate is the lovely **Azure Clouds Temple** (¥10; ◷8am-5pm), one of the oldest shrines in the city.

Best
Modern
Architecture

ARCHITECT: PAUL ANDREU, SUN XUEJUN/ALAMY ©

Few cities in the world can match Beijing's extraordinary mix of building styles – in the space of a few minutes' walking you can span an architectural narrative of six centuries or more. Beijing's modern architecture, from the grandiose, Socialist Realist designs of the 1950s to the daring, cutting-edge structures going up now, make for thrilling eye candy.

Best Controversial Buildings

CCTV Building (p91) You can't miss 'big underpants', a jaw-dropping structure that looms over the CBD and seemingly defies gravity.

National Centre for the Performing Arts (NCPA; p65) Nosing up from the ground like a huge reflective mushroom, the NCPA divides opinion like no other building in Beijing.

Post-1949

After the Communist Party's takeover of China in 1949, Soviet-inspired Socialist Realist architecture was the big thing. The vast edifices that line Tiananmen Square are the prime examples of this style of building.

1990s On

In the last decade, Beijing's city planners have looked West for inspiration and approved some truly radical structures. Check out the CCTV Tower for an example of how Beijing has embraced the architectural avant-garde.

Best Socialist Realist Architecture

Great Hall of the People (p32) A hulking monster of a building that encapsulates the lack of movement in China's political life over the last 60-odd years.

National Museum of China (p31) Taking up most of the east side of Tiananmen Square, this is another sombre monument to the power of the Communist Party.

Best
Markets

Markets in Beijing range from the hi-tech to household bric-a-brac laid out on the pavement. But no matter what they're selling – and you can find just about everything in the capital's markets – they provide some of the most fun shopping experiences in Beijing. Above all, they're places to pit your wits against some of the canniest hagglers you'll ever meet.

TRAVELASIA/GETTY IMAGES ©

Bargaining

Bargaining is not only advisable in markets but expected. Haggle hard – all vendors think foreigners are loaded – but remember to keep it friendly. The point of bargaining is not to screw the seller into the ground, but to find a mutually acceptable price. It always helps to smile.

☑ **Top Tip**

▶ The general rule in Beijing markets is to pay no more than half of the original price quoted. If the vendor won't budge, then just walking away often results in a rapid discount.

Best for Clothes

Sanlitun Yashow Clothing Market (p83) Everything from belts to shoes, via jackets, jeans and T-shirts.

Silk Market (p88) A legendary Beijing institution with some of the hardest hagglers of all.

Best for Antiques, Arts & Crafts

Panjiayuan Antique Market (p86) The most fun market in Beijing and well worth trawling for hidden treasures.

Beijing Curio City (p93) Antiques, as well as carpets and furniture, in a less touristy atmosphere than most markets in Beijing.

Best for Computers & Electronics

Centergate Como (p105) Vast seven-floor emporium with the lowest prices in town for gadgets.

Bainaohui (p83) Everything from gaming gear to software.

Best for Browsing

Hongqiao Pearl Market (p55) Pearls and more pearls, plus jade, jewellery, clothing and electronics.

Maliandao Tea Market (p69) For all the tea in China. Nearby are cheap tea sets.

Best Shopping

Shopping is one of Beijing's pleasures – whether you're looking for a unique souvenir, haggling over jewellery or just soaking up the atmosphere in the city's ever-increasing malls. Prices aren't as cheap as they used to be, but good deals are still paid for art, scrolls, silk, jewellery, jade and clothing.

DENNIS COX/ALAMY ©

Where to Start

For offbeat, fun souvenirs, try Nanluogu Xiang, while you'll find the trendiest and most upmarket malls in North and South Chaoyang. Head to Liulichang Xijie and Liulichang Dongjie for inks, paintings and scrolls, or to get a chop, a personalised ink stamp or seal, made. The nearby Dashilar area is home to some of Beijing's oldest stores.

Best Souvenirs

Shard Box Store (p88) Beautiful boxes and jewellery.

Grifted (p45) Quirky and cool gifts, most made locally.

Three Stone Kite Shop (p69) Kites by appointment to the emperors.

Yuehaixuan Musical Instrument Store (p69) Hand-made Chinese instruments.

Plastered 8 (p45) Ironic T-shirts with Beijing themes.

Rongbaozhai (p69) Calligraphy and ink scroll paintings.

Best Chinese Fashion

Five Colours Earth (p88) Tops, jackets and dresses with a traditional Chinese twist.

Ruifuxiang Silk (p69) The place to come for quality silk items.

Best Malls

Sanlitun Village (p83) The trendiest mall in town.

☑ Top Tips

▶ Be wary when buying antiques; it is illegal to take anything made before 1795 out of China without permission and there are many, many fakes out there.

▶ Upscale malls and shops will take credit cards. Everywhere else, it's cash only.

▶ Most malls and shops open from 9am to 9pm or later.

The Place (p88) Great outdoor area and mid-range brands.

China World Shopping Mall (p88) The top fashion names, as well as jewellery.

Best
Tours

Bike Beijing (康多自行车
租赁; ☎6526 5857; www
.bikebeijing.com; 34 Dong-
huangchenggen Nanjie 东
皇城根南街34号; ◷9am-
7pm; Ⓢ China Museum of
Art) Runs recommended
and safe half- and one-
day tours of Beijing by
bike, including tours
of imperial Beijing, the
hutong and out to the
Great Wall (p106). All
guides speak English and
they provide you with
helmets as well. You can
also rent bikes here.

Dandelion Hiking
(☎156 522 00950; www
.chinahiking.cn) Reputable
and friendly outfit that
specialises in hikes along
the Great Wall (p106), as
well to the Ming Tombs
(p109) and other areas
around Beijing. They do
one-day hikes (or you
can camp overnight), the
groups are never more

than 10 people and the
guides are knowledge-
able.

Beijing Sideways (☎139
110 34847; www.beijingside
ways.com) Fancy seeing
Beijing from the sidecar
of an old-school Chinese
motorbike? Then this
unique, French-run tour
company is for you. The
trips out to the Great
Wall (p106) are espe-
cially fun, but they do
two- and four-hour tours
of Beijing too. You can
also plan your own itiner-
ary and they'll take up to
20 people in a convoy.

China Culture Center
(☎6432 9341; www
.chinaculturecenter.org)
Long-standing organisa-
tion that runs tours of
the *hutong* by pedicab, as
well as themed cultural
tours to places like Maliandao Tea Market (p69)

TAO IMAGES LIMITED/GETTY IMAGES ©

☑ **Top Tip**

▶ Remember that
almost all hostels
run tours of Beijing
specifically designed
for Western travel-
lers. They're often
the easiest way to
see the Great Wall in
particular.

and art and architecture
visits. They can take you
round all Beijing's main
sights too. The walk-
ing tours to less-visited
parts of the capital come
recommended.

Best
Food

Food is an absolute obsession for the Chinese and eating out is the favourite social activity for Beijingers. With over 60,000 restaurants, and countless thousands of street-food stands, they're spoilt for choice and you will be too. Every one of China's numerous cuisines are on offer here, so you can eat your way across the country without ever leaving the capital.

DANIEL GASIENICA/GETTY IMAGES ©

Beijing Food

Chinese cuisine has four main schools, one for each compass point. Beijing food is classified as 'northern cuisine', which makes heavy use of wheat and millet, with noodles and steamed dumplings popular staples. Peking duck is the city's most famous dish. Beijingers, though, are equally enthusiastic about hotpot, which has Mongol origins, and the local street food, which involves anything that can be whipped up roadside or skewered on a stick. You'll see a lot of Sichuan (western China cuisine) restaurants in Beijing, as well as more esoteric places with food from far-off provinces.

Eating out in Beijing

Dining Chinese-style is a noisy, chaotic and often messy affair. Beijingers like to eat in big groups and they're at their most relaxed and gregarious when sitting around the dining table. Restaurants aren't judged by their decor or service; the only thing that matters is the food and the company. Most Chinese dishes are meant to be eaten communally, with everyone digging in with their chopsticks. A selection of meat, fish and vegetable dishes, both cold and hot, is the standard order. Don't worry about dropping food; you won't be the only one doing so.

Best Peking Duck

Beijing Dadong Roast Duck Restaurant (p42) Crispy, lean and delicious duck.

Liqun Roast Duck Restaurant (p54) Brilliant birds served in a traditional courtyard house.

Qianmen Quanjude Roast Duck Restaurant (p54) The most famous Peking duck restaurant in town and still one of the best.

Bianyifang (p55) Long-established and mostly tourist-free.

Duck de Chine (p78) Fancy-pants French meets Beijing duck.

Best Beijing

Najia Xiaoguan (p91) Dishes based on recipes from an old imperial cookbook.

Peking duck

Xiao Wang's Family Restaurant (p88) Home-style Beijing food.

Zuo Lin You She (p43) Proper locals joint: tasty grub and cheap as chips.

Best Dumplings

Duyichu (p55) Delicately-made *shaomai* here.

Din Tai Fung (p91) High-quality food in pleasant surroundings.

Baoyuan Dumpling Restaurant (p78) Multi-coloured dumplings!

Goubuli (p66) A multitude of traditional steamed dumplings.

Best International

Bei (p78) High-class and very trendy north Asian fusion.

Grill 79 (p93) Posh steakhouse in the skies.

4Corners (p65) Zingy Southeast Asian–style dishes.

Vineyard Café (p43) Has Western comfort food and a laidback atmosphere.

Hutong Pizza (p66) Some of the best pies in town.

Best Hutong Restaurants

Dali Courtyard (p42) Fantastic, romantic setting and different dishes chosen by the chef each day.

Tan Hua Lamb BBQ (p43) Grill your own leg of lamb at this raucous venue.

Baihe Vegetarian Restaurant (p43) Top-notch veggie dishes in soothing, spiritual surroundings.

Source (p43) Swish Sichuan with the spices toned down in a cool courtyard house.

Best Regional Chinese

Lost Heaven (p55) Folk cuisine from the southwest in an upmarket setting.

Golden Peacock (p105) Southeast Asia meets China at this very authentic Dai restaurant.

Herbal Café (p79) MSG-free Hong Kong favourites.

Yuelu Shanwu (p65) Fiery Hunan dishes and a great view.

Best
Drinking & Nightlife

LANE OATEY/BLUE JEAN IMAGES/GETTY IMAGES ©

It's amazing to contemplate, but 20 years ago there weren't any bars in Beijing, save for a few in hotels for foreigners, and nor were there any nightclubs. Now, though, the city's drinking and nightlife scene has exploded. You can sip fancy cocktails in a stylish setting, or neck beers in a hip *hutong* bar, and there are numerous options for dancing the night away.

Choose Your Scene

Just as the number of bars has increased dramatically, so they have spread all across Beijing. Sanlitun in north Chaoyang remains the nightlife hub, especially for cocktail bars and clubs, but the *hutong* of Dongcheng North are now packed with cool cafes and laidback bars. Nanluogu Xiang and the alleys behind the Drum and Bell Towers are good spots to head to.

South Chaoyang is home to high-end venues for the CBD crowd, while the Wudaokou neighbourhood in Haidian has a buzzing student scene centred on the bars and cafes on and off Chengfu Lu. The free English-language listings magazines (p141) are the best way to find out about hot new drinking spots.

Drink Like a Local

Although many Beijingers would rather sing karaoke (p80), or share a ¥3 beer and some street food, than drop ¥60 on a cocktail, rising incomes and the more Westernised attitude of young Chinese means the locals are increasingly heading to bars. The many places around the Houhai lakes are especially popular in the summer, while more and more Beijingers are partying in the bars and clubs of Sanlitun.

Best Cocktail Bars

Apothecary (p79) No standing at the bar, but some of the finest mixologists in Beijing.

Migas (p79) Deservedly popular hangout, especially in the summer when the roof terrace gets rammed.

George's (p74) Excellent drinks and a comfortably trendy atmosphere.

Q Bar (p80) Long-standing place that's still one of the most amenable spots in town.

d Lounge (p80) Fashionable industrial-style setting with solid drinks and staff with attitude.

Best Hutong Bars

Mao Mao Chong (p44) Laid-back venue with proper mixed drinks, a

World of Suzie Wong (p81)

good range of beers and a nice line in pizzas.

El Nido (p44) One of the bars of the moment with a huge choice of brews; fine on summer nights when you can sit outside.

12SqM (p44) Not as compact as it once was, but still one of the friendliest bars in town.

Bed Bar (p67) Cool spot spread over a number of traditional courtyards and, yes, it has beds.

Modernista (p44) Hipster hang-out with live music and film screenings.

Drum & Bell (p40) Great roof terrace for lazy Sunday-afternoon drinks.

Best to Impress

Atmosphere (p93) Beijing's loftiest bar: great view, decent cocktails and live jazz.

Glen (p74) A bar for connoisseurs of fine cocktails and superb single malts. We like the shaved ice cubes.

Mesh (p74) Gay-friendly on Thursdays, but a beautiful-people hangout any night of the week.

LAN (p93) Over-the-top design which makes for a unique drinking backdrop.

Best Cafes

Stone Boat (p91) Peaceful cafe by day, chilled bar by night and a great pit stop at any time.

Bookworm (p80) One of the hubs of Beijing cultural life. Part cafe and part library, there's no need to bring a book.

Lush (p102) Still the epicentre of the student crowd in Wudaokou and it never closes.

Best Clubs

Haze (p92) The current hot spot and home to the best local spinners.

Cargo (p74) Often hosts big-name DJs. Much more of a locals' place than other clubs.

Destination (p80) Beijing's only official gay club is always busy.

World of Suzie Wong (p81) It's been around forever and the crowd can be dodgy, but it still packs them in.

Best **Entertainment**

Visitors are spoiled for choice when it comes to performances in Beijing. Not only are there the still-thriving traditional Chinese arts – Peking opera and acrobatics – but there are an increasing number of live-music venues showcasing both local and foreign acts.

DBIMAGES/ALAMY ©

Acrobatics

Beijing's acrobatics troupes are some of the best in the country. There's nothing quite like seeing young contortionists turn themselves inside out and upside down, while spinning plates on the ends of long sticks, or balancing on poles. And they've been doing it for a while – as far back as the Warring States Period (roughly 475–221 BC) there are mentions of dagger-juggling and stilt-walking.

These days, professional Chinese acrobats undergo the same rigorous training as future sports stars. Gifted children as young as five or six are singled out and enrolled in schools run by the various acrobatic companies. And, like sport, it is a short career. The typical acrobat retires from performing sometime in their thirties.

Best Live Music

Yugong Yishan (p44)
Local and foreign bands, as well as electronic knob-twiddlers, take to the stage at this excellent venue.

East Shore Jazz Café (p68) *The* place to hang out with Beijing's jazzers.

National Centre for the Performing Arts (NCPA; p65) Head here for classical music concerts, ballet, opera and theatre.

Best Acrobatics & Peking Opera

Tianqiao Acrobatics Theatre (p67) Perhaps the best show in town at this hundred-year-old-plus venue.

Huguang Guild Hall (p68) Superb historic venue to take in a traditional Peking opera show.

Universal Theatre (Heaven & Earth Theatre; p81) Home to the Chinese National Acrobatics Troupe.

Chaoyang Theatre (p81) Spectacular daily acrobatic performances and occasional opera shows too.

Best
For Kids

Beijing Zoo & Beijing Aquarium (北京动物园、北京海洋馆; 137 Xizhimenwai Dajie 西直门外大街137号; zoo ¥15, panda house ¥5 extra, zoo & aquarium adult/child ¥130/70; ☉7.30am-6pm Apr-Oct, to 5pm Nov-Mar; ⓢBeijing Zoo) It's a long way from being the most ethically sound zoo on the planet, but it does have pandas and what kid doesn't like a fluffy black-and-white panda? Also on the same site is the impressive aquarium, which has daily aquatic animal displays.

Happy Magic Water Park (水立方嬉水乐园; Olympic Green, off Beichen Lu 北辰路奥林匹克公园内; water park adult/child ¥200/160, swimming only ¥50; ☉10am-9pm; ⓢOlympic Green) Beijing's largest indoor water park is housed in this otherworldly, bubble-like

structure (one of the venues for the 2008 Olympics). Kids love the warren of neon plastic slides, tunnels, water jets and pools.

China Puppet Theatre (中国木偶剧院; ☎6425 4847; cnr Anhua Xili & North 3rd Ring Rd 北三环中路安华西里; puppet shows 10am-2.30pm; tickets ¥100; ⓢHepingxiqiao, then ➌104, 101 or 特8) Shadow play, puppetry, music and dance events on weekends at this fairy-tale castle of a building. There are two theatres here; the puppet shows are always in the smaller one. The shows aren't in English but are easy to follow.

Toys City (红桥天乐玩具市场; 36 Hongqiao Lu 红桥路36号; ☉8.30am-7pm; ⓢTiantandongmen) Located in the building directly behind the Hongqiao Pearl Market (p55),

CHINA PHOTOS/STRINGER/GETTY IMAGES ©

☑ **Top Tips**

▶ Nappies (diapers), baby bottles and formula milk are widely available at supermarkets.

▶ Kids usually pay half price at tourist sights. Tots under 120cm in height are free for sights and public transport.

this place is stuffed to the gills with toys that whiz, whir, beep and flash, as well soft toys, cars, model kits, Wii sets, PlayStations and computer games.

Best
For Free

ICONOTEC/ALAMY/GETTY IMAGES ©

Beijing may not appear at first sight to be a city overburdened with freebies. But dig a little and there are a plethora of places to see, things to do and worthwhile experiences to be had which don't involve cash changing hands.

Best Sights

798 Art District (p72) It's free to peruse the galleries. But only true skinflints will consider walking here.

Tiananmen Square (p30) Stroll with the hordes, or catch the flag-raising and lowering ceremonies at dawn and dusk.

Chairman Mao Memorial Hall (p31) It doesn't cost a *mao* to shuffle reverently past the Great Helmsman's mummified remains.

Foreign Legation Quarter (p112) Enjoy a complimentary walk past the imposing European architecture of this area.

Ming City Wall Ruins Park (p53) The sole remaining section of Beijing's city walls; this unique slice of history comes gratis.

Wuta Temple (p102) Free admission Wednesday for the first 200 visitors.

Best Museums

Capital Museum (p64) The best museum in the city and it's on the house.

National Museum of China (p31) A free crash course in 5000 years of Chinese history.

Best Activities

Houhai (p64) Join the locals as they promenade around the lakes, or play them at table tennis.

Hutong (p46) Walk your shoes off through myriad ancient lanes that criss-cross central Beijing.

Top Tips

▶ To get into the museums and sights that don't charge, you'll need to show your passport.

▶ Many parks levy only a nominal ¥2 entrance fee.

Best Parks

Jingshan Park (p41) Climb the hill for free views over the Forbidden City.

Ritan Park (p91) A peaceful oasis in the heart of the busy CBD.

Survival Guide

Survival Guide

Before You Go

When to Go

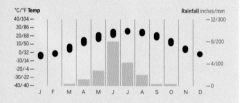

→ Winter (Nov–Mar)
Below freezing temperatures and sometimes snow. Air pollution can be bad. Far fewer visitors in town, so sights are crowd-free.

→ Spring (Apr–May)
The short spring is pleasant, but tourist numbers start to increase.

→ Summer (June–Aug)
Very hot and humid; hotels are booked out and the main sights are packed.

→ Autumn (Sep–Oct)
Clear skies; the best weather of the year. Domestic visitors descend on the capital in the first week of October.

Book Your Stay

☑ **Top Tip** During the three major Chinese public holidays (p141), hotel prices jump dramatically and accommodation is hard to find. Book ahead.

➡ Dongcheng North is the handiest area to stay in for sights, but Xicheng and North Chaoyang are also popular.

➡ For a hotel with real Beijing atmosphere, go for the growing coterie of courtyard hotels, mostly located in traditional *hutong* neighbourhoods.

➡ Beijing has an increasing number of chain hotels; they are bland but cleaner and more modern than the many old-school two- and three-star hotels.

➡ Hostel staff will speak the best English and their visitor information and tours are generally superior to other hotels.

➡ Outside of the peak tourist season, many hotels slash their listed rates by as much as 50%. Don't be shy about asking for a discount.

Useful Websites

Lonely Planet (www.lonely planet.com/china/beijing) Author recommendation views and online booking.

Ctrip (www.ctrip.com) Good for discount hotel reservations.

Hostelbookers (www .hostelbookers.com) Big range of hostels and guesthouses.

China Homestay (www .chinahomestay.org) Local families who host guests.

Best Budget

Red Lantern House West Yard (www.redlantern house.com) Charming guesthouse in the middle of hutong-land.

Qianmen Hostel (www .qianmenhostel.net) Heritage hostel and traveller-friendly favourite.

Beijing Downtown Backpackers (www.back packingchina.com) Basic but clean rooms in the heart of trendy Nanluogu Xiang (p42).

Three-Legged Frog Hostel (3legs@threelegged froghostel.com) Crazy

name, but decent rooms around a cute courtyard.

Beijing P-Loft Youth Hostel (ploft@yahoo.cn) Efficient and amenable place that's tucked away but still close to the sights.

Best Midrange

The Orchid (www.the orchidbeijing.com) Tasteful rooms at this peaceful courtyard hotel.

The Emperor (www.theem peror.com.cn) Pleasingly off-beat hotel slap next door to the Forbidden City.

Hotel Kapok (www.hotel kapok.com) Midrange cool for designer types.

Bamboo Garden Hotel (www.bbgh.com.cn) Elegant, hushed and historic courtyard hotel.

Park Plaza (www.parkplaza .com/beijingcn) Good value, friendly, comfortable and a solid location.

Best Top End

DuGe (www.dugecourtyard .com) Exquisite designer courtyard hotel; only six rooms.

St Regis (www.stregis.com /beijing) Sumptuous in every way and fantastic restaurants.

Ritz-Carlton Beijing, Financial Street (www .ritzcarlton.com) Wonderful service and luxurious, spacious rooms.

Courtyard 7 (www .courtyard7.com) Immaculate rooms and a winning hutong location.

Opposite House (www .theoppositehouse.com) Striking building and top-drawer trendy.

Arriving in Beijing

☑ **Top Tip** For the best way to get to your accom-modation, see p17.

From Beijing Capital International Airport

➡ The Airport Express (机场快轨) links terminals 2 and 3 at the airport to Beijing's subway system at Sanyuanqiao station (Line 10) and Dongzhi-men station (Lines 2 and 13). Tickets cost ¥25 one way; it's a 30-minute ride into town. Frequent trains depart terminal 3 from 6.21am to 10.51pm;

terminal 2, 6.35am to 11.10pm. Note that the subway service runs til around 11pm.

➡ There are 10 different routes for the airport shuttle bus (机场巴士). Buses leave from all three terminals and run 5am to midnight. Tickets cost ¥16 one way. Line 1 runs to the CBD and South Chaoyang. Take Line 3 for Dongzhimen and Dongcheng North.

➡ A taxi (using its meter) should cost ¥80 to ¥100 from the airport to the city centre, including the ¥15 airport expressway toll; bank on it taking 40 minutes to one hour to get into town. Ignore taxi touts and take an official cab. Have the name of your

hotel written down in Chinese to show the driver, as very few speak English.

From Beijing Train Station

➡ International trains from Mongolia, North Korea, Russia and Vietnam arrive at the Beijing Train Station (北京站), the capital's main terminus, which is on Line 2 of the subway.

From Beijing West Train Station

➡ Trains from Hong Kong arrive at the vast Beijing West Train Station (北京西站), which is on Line 9 of the subway.

Getting Around

Subway

☑ **Best for**... getting around the city quickly and safely.

➡ Beijing's subway system is massive, modern, easy to use, efficient, safe and ever-expanding. There are currently 15 lines, all numbered.

➡ Trains run from 6am to 11pm, tickets cost ¥2 for a single journey anywhere on the network.

➡ To recognise a subway station (地铁站; *ditie zhan*) look for the subway symbol: a blue English capital 'D' with a circle around it.

Bicycle

☑ **Best for**... exploring the *hutong* and central Beijing.

➡ Renting a bike (租自行车; *zuzixingche*) is a great way to get around traffic-clogged Beijing, especially the *hutong*. Be aware that cars will not give way for bikes.

➡ Most hostels rent bikes typically for ¥30 a day for a standard town bike. Bike Beijing (p127) is a good place to rent better quality bikes and helmets Many places around the Houhai lakes (p64) rent bikes for ¥10 an hour, ¥200 deposit.

➡ By the time you read this, Beijing's new bike-sharing scheme should be in operation: 20,000 bikes available at 500 kiosks around town, with a ¥200 deposit; first 30 minutes free, after that a bargain ¥1 per hour.

Travel Cards

You can get a travel card (交通一卡通; *jiaotong yikatong*) for the subway for a ¥20 refundable deposit. They won't make your journey any cheaper, but you avoid having to queue for tickets. And they do get you a 60% discount on all bus journeys inside Beijing.

Taxi

☑ **Best for**... long journeys and late at night.

➡ Taxis (出租车; *chuzuche*) are everywhere, but finding one can be a problem during rush hour, rainstorms and between 8pm and 10pm, when people are heading home after dinner.

➡ Flag fall is ¥10 for the first 3km. After that it's ¥2 per kilometre. Drivers also add a ¥3 fuel surcharge. Rates increase slightly at night.

➡ Few drivers speak English; have the name and address of where you're going written down in Chinese characters. Always remember to keep your hotel's business card on you so you can get home at the end of the night.

➡ Most Beijing taxi drivers are honest. If they refuse to use the meter (打表; *dabiao*), get out and find another one.

➡ Taxis can be hired for out-of-town trips like the Great Wall (p106), but you will have to agree a price (but not pay) beforehand.

Bus

☑ **Best for**... travelling to places not on the subway.

➡ Beijing's buses (公共汽车; *gonggong qiche*) are numerous and go everywhere. Tickets cost ¥1.

➡ Non-Chinese speakers can find it a challenge to get from A to B successfully. It's best to have your destination written down in Chinese characters to show the bus conductor, who can tell you where to get off.

➡ Heavy traffic means bus journeys are slow, and they are always packed.

Essential Information

Business Hours

☑ **Top Tip** Many museums and sights stop selling tickets 30 minutes before closing.

➡ Exceptions to the following hours are noted in individual listings.

➡ **Bars and cafes** 11am–2am Mon-Sun

➡ **Internet cafes** 24hr Mon-Sun

➡ **Offices, banks & government departments** 9am-5pm or 6pm Mon-Fri

➡ **Restaurants** 10.30am-10pm Mon-Sun

Discounts

➡ Children under a certain height (normally 120cm) get in free or for half price at sights, as do seniors over the age of 65.

➡ Produce a student card or an **ISIC card** (www.isiccard.com) and you may get into sights for half price.

Electricity

➡ Electricity is 220V/50 Hz. Beijing plugs vary, so you'll see up to four different sorts around town. Adaptors are available to buy in Beijing.

220V/50Hz

220V/50Hz

Emergencies

→ **Ambulance** ☏120

→ **Fire** ☏119

→ **Police** ☏110

Internet

→ All hostels and most hotels have internet access, sometimes for a small charge. Many now have free wi-fi access too.

→ Cafes and bars with wi-fi are widespread in Beijing.

→ Internet cafes (网吧; *wangba*) are numerous but often squirreled away in basements or on the upper floors of anonymous buildings;

keep your eyes peeled for the Chinese characters. Standard rates are ¥3 to ¥5 per hour.

→ You will need to show your passport to use an internet cafe.

→ The Chinese government routinely blocks websites it considers sensitive. They include social media sites like Facebook, Twitter and YouTube. To access these, you will need to install a VPN (virtual private network) on your laptop or phone.

Money

☑ **Top Tip** Counterfeit money is common in China. Foreigners are prime targets for fake bills. Don't be shy about handing suspicious money back. Vendors will usually hand you a different bill without a fuss.

→ Chinese currency is called Renminbi (RMB), or 'people's money'. Its basic unit is the *yuan* (¥), called *kuai* in spoken Chinese. There are also smaller, almost worthless now, denominations of *jiao* and *fen*.

→ **ATMs** Most banks in Beijing accept foreign ATM and credit cards connected to Plus, Cir-

rus, Visa, MasterCard and American Express, although there will be a small charge levied (either by your bank or the local one).

→ The ATMs of the Bank of China and the Industrial and Commercial Bank of China (ICBC) are the most reliable choices for foreign card-users.

→ **Credit cards** Most four- and five-star hotels, upmarket restaurants and shops, major malls and department stores accept credit cards. Everywhere else, you need cash.

→ You can get cash advances on credit cards from the Bank of China, though you will pay a steep 4% commission.

→ **Money changers** Foreign currency can be changed at the Bank of China, ICBC, CITIC Bank, the China Construction Bank, at the airport, and at some large department stores. You'll always need your passport. Hotels normally give the official exchange rate but may add a small commission.

→ Hang onto your exchange receipts; you may be asked to show them when you change your remaining RMB back into another currency.

→ **Tipping** Not standard in Beijing. Posh restaurants and hotels will tack on a 10% to 15% service charge; nowhere else is it expected. Taxi drivers do not expect tips.

→ **Travellers Cheques** If issued by leading banks and issuing agencies like American Express and Visa, they can be cashed at the Bank of China and ICBC, exchange desks at the airport and upscale hotels (if you're a guest).

Newspapers & Magazines

→ Check the English-language listings magazines *The Beijinger* and *Time Out Beijing* for the latest entertainment hot spots. Both list the addresses in Chinese of many restaurants, bars and clubs, so you can show them to taxi drivers.

→ There are two state-run English-language newspapers: *China Daily*, a broadsheet, and *Global Times*, a tabloid. Neither are exciting reads.

Public Holidays

☑ **Top Tip** Chinese New Year and National Day

are the start of week-long holidays; 1 May marks the beginning of a three-day holiday. Sights get very crowded at these times and hotel prices shoot up.

New Year's Day
1 January

Spring Festival (Chinese New Year) Generally falls in January and February: 10 February 2013, 31 January 2014

International Women's Day 8 March

Tomb Sweeping Festival
5 May

International Labour Day 1 May

Youth Day 4 May

International Children's Day 1 June

Anniversary of the Founding of the Chinese Communist Party
1 July

Anniversary of the Founding of the People's Liberation Army
1 August

Moon Festival End of September

National Day 1 October

Safe Travel

→ Beijing is one of the safest cities of its size in the

world. Serious or violent crimes against foreigners and visitors are rare.

→ Road safety should be your biggest concern. Be aware that traffic goes in all directions all the time and will not give way for pedestrians.

→ Do watch out for pickpockets on public transport.

→ At the airport, taxi sharks wait to lure weary travellers into taking illegal cabs costing ¥300 or more. Always take an official taxi.

→ A common scam in the Tiananmen Square area involves English-speaking young women inviting you to participate in a traditional teahouse ceremony. They will disappear before the end and you will be left with a bill running into hundreds of dollars.

→ Avoid so-called 'art students' who want you to view their work: they're not students and they will try to sell you overpriced rubbish.

Telephone

☑ **Top Tip** Pick up a local SIM card (¥60 to ¥100) from one of the many China Mobile or China Unicom shops; it's the cheapest way to use your mobile phone.

→ International and domestic calls are easily made from your hotel room or public phones. Local calls from hotel rooms are mostly free (check first), but international calls are expensive; it's better to use a phonecard.

→ Local calls can be made from public phones (usually yellow or orange), at newspaper stands and hole-in-the-wall shops. You pay the owner when you finish.

→ The country code to use to access China is ☎86.

→ To call a number in Beijing from abroad, dial the international access code (☎00 in the UK, ☎011 in the USA and so on), dial the country code (☎86) and then the area code for Beijing (☎010), dropping the first zero, and then dial the local number.

→ For telephone calls within the same city, drop the area code.

→ **Mobile Phones** Your cell phone from home should work in Beijing (check it's been unlocked for overseas use before leaving).

→ Credit-charging cards (充值卡; *chongzhi ka*) for local SIM cards are sold at most convenience stores and newspaper stands in ¥50 or ¥100 denominations. Calls are less than ¥1 a minute.

→ Phone cards, or IP cards (internet phone; IP卡; *IP ka*), are best for making international calls and come in various denominations.

→ Most cards either have English-language instructions on them, or an English-language option once you dial the card number.

→ IC (integrated circuit) cards (IC卡; *IC ka*), for domestic calls, can be used at most public phones.

→ IP and IC cards are sold at newspaper stands, small shops, China Telecom offices and some hotels.

Toilets

→ Public toilets are everywhere in Beijing, but most are squat versions and are often pungent and primitive. Carry your own toilet paper or tissues (available in every small shop).

→ If you see a waste basket next to the toilet, that's where you should throw the toilet paper.

→ Make a beeline for fast-food outlets, top-end hotels and department stores for more hygienic alternatives.

Dos & Don'ts

→ In general, the Chinese do not stand on ceremony.

→ Beijingers are getting better at queuing, but it's a work in progress; expect some scrums.

→ The Asian concept of 'face', and maintaining it at all times, means losing your temper in public is not good form. Smiling your way out of problems is always the best option.

→ Avoid discussing politics with the locals.

→ When eating, don't point your chopsticks at people and don't stick them vertically in a bowl of rice; it's an omen of death.

➡ The symbol for men is 男 (*nan*) and women is 女 (*nu*).

Tourist Information

➡ Staff at the chain of **Beijing Tourist Information Centers** (北京旅游 咨询; ⏰ 9am-5pm) around town generally have limited English-language skills and are not always helpful, but you can grab a free tourist map of town.

➡ Your best sources of information will be your accommodation and other travellers.

Travellers with Disabilities

➡ Beijing is a challenge for anyone with limited mobility.

➡ Take a lightweight wheelchair that can be folded up if necessary.

➡ There are few elevators (lifts), plus escalators in subway stations usually only go up.

➡ Streets are overcrowded and uneven, forcing wheelchair users onto the road itself.

➡ Getting around sights is difficult – ramps are rare.

➡ Travellers with sight, hearing or mobility dis-abilities will also need to be extremely cautious of the traffic, which does not yield to pedestrians.

Visas

➡ Visas are required for everyone visiting mainland China, bar nationals of Brunei, Japan and Singapore.

➡ A standard 30-day, single-entry visa is readily available from Chinese embassies and consulates worldwide and usually takes three to five working days.

Language

Mandarin Chinese – or Pǔtōnghuà (common speech), as it's referred to by the Chinese – can be written using the Roman alphabet. This system is known as Pinyin; in the following phrases we have provided both Mandarin script and Pinyin.

Mandarin has 'tonal' quality – the raising and lowering of pitch on certain syllables. There are four tones in Mandarin, plus a fifth 'neutral' tone that you can all but ignore. In Pinyin the tones are indicated with accent marks on vowels: **ā** (high), **á** (rising), **ǎ** (falling-rising), **à** (falling).

To enhance your trip with a phrasebook, visit **lonelyplanet.com**. Lonely Planet iPhone phrasebooks are available through the Apple App store.

Basics

Hello.	你好。	Nǐhǎo.
Goodbye.	再见。	Zàijiàn.
How are you?	你好吗?	Nǐhǎo ma?
Fine.	好。	Hǎo.
And you?	你呢?	Nǐ ne?
Please ...	请……	Qǐng ...
Thank you.	谢谢你。	Xièxie nǐ.
Excuse me.	劳驾。	Láojià.
Sorry.	对不起。	Duìbùqǐ.
Yes.	是。	Shì.
No.	不是。	Bùshì.

Do you speak English?
你会说
英文吗?
Nǐ huìshuō
Yīngwén ma?

I don't understand.
我不明白。　　Wǒ bù míngbái.

Eating & Drinking

I'd like ...
我要……　　Wǒ yào ...

a table for two	一张两个人的桌子	yīzhāng liǎngge rén de zhuōzi
the drink list	酒水单	jiǔshuǐ dān
the menu	菜单	càidān
beer	啤酒	píjiǔ
coffee	咖啡	kāfēi

I don't eat ...
我不吃……　　Wǒ bùchī ...

fish	鱼	yú
poultry	家禽	jiāqín
red meat	牛羊肉	niúyángròu

Cheers!
干杯!　　Gānbēi!

That was delicious.
真好吃。　　Zhēn hǎochī.

The bill, please!
买单!　　Mǎidān!

Shopping

I'd like to buy ...
我想买……　　Wǒ xiǎng mǎi ...

I'm just looking.
我先看看。　　Wǒ xiān kànkan.

How much is it?
多少钱？　　　Duōshǎo qián?

That's too expensive.
太贵了。　　　Tàiguì le.

Can you lower the price?
能便宜　　　　Néng piányi
一点吗？　　　yīdiǎn ma?

Emergencies

Help!　救命！　　Jiùmìng!

Go away!　走开！　　Zǒukāi!

Call a doctor!
请叫医生来！　Qǐng jiào yīshēng lái!

Call the police!
请叫警察！　　Qǐng jiào jǐngchá!

I'm lost.
我迷路了。　　Wǒ mílù le.

I'm sick.
我生病了。　　Wǒ shēngbìng le.

Where are the toilets?
厕所在哪儿？　Cèsuǒ zài nǎr?

Time & Numbers

What time is it?
现在几点钟？　Xiànzài jǐdiǎn zhōng?

It's (10) o'clock.
(十)点钟。　　(Shí)diǎn zhōng.

Half past (10).
(十)点三十分。　(Shí)diǎn sānshífēn.

morning	早上	zǎoshang
afternoon	下午	xiàwǔ
evening	晚上	wǎnshàng
yesterday	昨天	zuótiān
today	今天	jīntiān
tomorrow	明天	míngtiān

1	一	yī
2	二/两	èr/liǎng
3	三	sān
4	四	sì
5	五	wǔ
6	六	liù
7	七	qī
8	八	bā
9	九	jiǔ
10	十	shí

Transport & Directions

Where's ...?
……在哪儿？　... zài nǎr?

What's the address?
地址在哪儿？　Dìzhǐ zài nǎr?

How do I get there?
怎么走？　　　Zěnme zǒu?

How far is it?
有多远？　　　Yǒu duō yuǎn?

Can you show me on the map?
请帮我找　　　Qǐng bāngwǒ zhǎo
它在地图上　　tā zài dìtú shàng
的位置。　　　de wèizhi.

When's the next bus?
下一趟车　　　Xià yītàng chē
几点走？　　　jǐdiǎn zǒu?

A ticket to ...
一张到　　　　Yīzhāng dào
……的票。　　... de piào.

Does it stop at ...?
在……能下　　Zài ... néng xià
车吗？　　　　chē ma?

I want to get off here.
我想这儿下车。　Wǒ xiǎng zhèr xiàchē.

Behind the Scenes

Send Us Your Feedback

We love to hear from travellers – your comments help make our books better. We read every word, and we guarantee that your feedback goes straight to the authors. Visit **lonelyplanet.com/contact** to submit your updates and suggestions.

Note: We may edit, reproduce and incorporate your comments in Lonely Planet products such as guidebooks, websites and digital products, so let us know if you don't want your comments reproduced or your name acknowledged. For a copy of our privacy policy visit lonelyplanet.com/privacy.

Our Readers

Many thanks to the travellers who used the last edition and wrote to us with helpful hints, useful advice and interesting anecdotes:

Melissa Ajero, Heo Junyoung, Jane Kypreos, Nora Leonardi, Kee Woei Ng, Yuma Ohkura, Hanna Pehkonen, Wai Ching Yeung.

David's Thanks

Special gratitude goes to Li Xinying for her invaluable assistance and to Daniel McCrohan for his sterling work on the *Beijing* city guide. Thanks to everyone who passed on tips, whether knowingly or unwittingly. Thanks also to Emily Wolman, Martine Power, Kathleen Munnelly and Diana Von Holdt at Lonely Planet.

Acknowledgments

Cover photograph: Summer Palace, Beijing; Best View Stock/Getty Images

This Book

This 3rd edition of Lonely Planet's *Pocket Beijing* guidebook was researched and written by David Eimer, who also wrote the previous edition. This guidebook was commissioned in Lonely Planet's Oakland office, and produced by the following:

Commissioning Editors Kathleen Munnelly, Emily K Wolman **Coordinating Editors** Kate James, Erin Richards **Coordinating Cartographer** Valentina Kremenchutskaya **Coordinating Layout Designer** Carlos Solarte **Managing Editor** Martine Power **Senior Editor** Catherine Naghten **Managing Cartographers** Corey Hutchison, Adrian Persoglia **Managing Layout Designer** Chris Girdler

Assisting Editor Evan Jones **Cover Research** Naomi Parker **Internal Image Research** Nicholas Colicchia, Kylie McLaughlin **Language Content** Branislava Vladisavljevic **Thanks** Barbara Delissen, Ryan Evans, Mark Griffiths, Wayne Murphy, Trent Paton, Jessica Rose, Phillip Tang, Diana Von Holdt, Gerard Walker.

Index

See also separate subindexes for:

❌ **Eating p149**

🍷 **Drinking p150**

🎭 **Entertainment p150**

🛍 **Shopping p150**

Our Writer

David Eimer

David first came to China in 1988, when both Westerners and cars were in short supply. After abandoning the idea of the law as a career and working as a freelance journalist in London and LA, he moved to Beijing in 2005 just in time to catch its emergence as a true world city. During his seven years living in Beijing, David travelled to almost every province in China, contributing to the last three editions of Lonely Planet's *China* guide. He has also coauthored the last three editions of the *Beijing* guide and wrote the previous edition of this book. David is currently based in Bangkok, and misses Beijing food and the *hutong*.

Published by Lonely Planet Publications Pty Ltd
ABN 36 005 607 983
3rd edition – April 2013
ISBN 978 1 74179 962 0

© Lonely Planet 2013   Photographs © as indicated 2013
10 9 8 7 6 5 4 3 2 1
Printed in Singapore